THE GLUCOSE COOKBOOK

Change Your Eating Routine with these Delicious Recipes to Energize, Heal, and Master Dinner Preparation Tips for the Best Nutrition and Glucose Control.

MICHELLE INCHAUSPE

Copyright © 2023 by Michelle Inchauspe

All rights reserved. No part of this book may be reproduced or transmitted in any form or by any means, electronic or mechanical, including photocopying, recording or by any information storage and retrieval system, without written permission from the author, except for the inclusion of brief quotations in a review.

This book is intended for informational purposes only and should not be considered a substitute for professional medical advice, diagnosis, or treatment. Always seek the advice of your physician or other qualified healthcare provider with any questions you may have regarding a medical condition.

FOREWORD

"The Glucose Goddess Cookbook" is something I'm very excited to introduce. As a certified diabetes educator and registered dietitian, I have witnessed firsthand how crucial a nutritious diet is for controlling blood sugar levels and avoiding chronic illnesses.

It is crucial to develop a conscious relationship with the food we eat in a world where processed meals and sugary temptations are everywhere. This cookbook provides a wide variety of recipes to help your journey, whether you are treating diabetes, trying to prevent glucose-related health complications, or simply adopting a healthier lifestyle.

You'll find breakfast creations that give your day energy and nourishment, lunchtime favorites that make you feel full and energized, dinner specialties that turn every meal into a celebration, and delicious desserts that sate your sweet tooth without jeopardizing your health in these pages.

The Glucose Goddess Cookbook is more than just a collection of culinary creations; it's also a manual for comprehending how food affects your body and psyche.

You will learn how to make informed decisions, swap out high-carb foods, and adopt cooking methods that support glucose control through educational insights and helpful advice.

May you enjoy the process of creating healthful meals as you set out on your culinary journey and come to understand the importance of nourishing your body from the inside out.

Keep in mind that every dish you make is a reflection of your love and self-care. May you enjoy the voyage of tasty and glucose-friendly cooking while accomplishing your health objectives with the help of this cookbook, which you can rely on.

I wish you good health, happiness, and a lifetime of delicious meals!

Sincerely,
Michelle Inchauspe
Qualified Diabetic Educator and Registered Dietitian.

PREFACE

I couldn't help but be profoundly motivated as I set out to write this cookbook with a deep desire to use the transformative power of food to positively touch the lives of people.

The Glucose Goddess Cookbook is the result of my quest to understand the complex relationship between diet and health, and it is my sincere wish that these pages may be a beacon of hope for you as you travel towards perfect health. After seeing the difficulties people had controlling their blood sugar, I believed it was my duty to develop a tool that would not only meet their dietary demands but also celebrate the pleasure of food. I have compiled a compilation of 100 recipes with painstaking research, professional advice, and a dash of culinary genius that perfectly captures flavor, nutrition, and balance.

This cookbook aims to provide you with knowledge, help you understand the secrets of glucose, and give you useful tools for making wise decisions. Each recipe is skillfully created to nurture your body and enrich your culinary experience, from energizing morning treats to hearty lunchtime favorites, magnificent dinner specialties to guilt-free sweets, and refreshing drinks to nourishing snacks.

However, this book explores the art of cooking with glucose in mind, going beyond simple meals. There are suggestions for cooking methods that promote blood sugar control while enhancing the flavor of each dish, portion control, meal planning, and component replacement.

May you enjoy the pleasures of cooking as you set out on this path, embrace the availability of healthful products, and take satisfaction in taking care of your body, mind, and spirit. May the Glucose Goddess Cookbook become a dependable friend in your kitchen, a source of ideas, and proof of the significant positive effects conscious eating can have on your health.

I appreciate you coming along on this gastronomic journey with me. Let's work together to realize the power of food to heal, nourish, and inspire as we adopt a healthy, glucose-friendly lifestyle.

Sincerely,
Michelle Inchauspe, RD, CDE.

CONTENTS

Copyright © 2023 by Michelle Inchauspe 2
FOREWORD 3
PREFACE 6
CONTENTS 9
INTRODUCTION 12
CHAPTER 1 18
What's Glucose **Again?** 18
How Your Body Produces Glucose 21
The Capacity for Energy 22
Hyperglycemia and Diabetes 24
Supplies of Glucose 27
The Significance of Glucose to the Body 28
Knowledge of Glucose and Health Effects ... 32

Choosing to Live a Balanced and Glucose-Friendly Lifestyle 36

Hacks on how to control Blood Sugar 40

CHAPTER 2 46

Morning Delights 46

CHAPTER 3 84

CHAPTER 4 106

Dinner Cuisine 106

CHAPTER 5 146

Filling Snacks 146

CHAPTER 6 178

Enticing Desserts 178

CHAPTER 7 204

Drinks and Beverages 204

CHAPTER 8 212

Hydration beyond Water 212

How to Maintain Body Hydration 214

CHAPTER 9 220

BONUS FEATURES 220

Food Shopping Guide: 220

Filling Your Cooler and Storeroom for Success
.... 220

Cooking Techniques and Kitchen Tips 225

Dinner Planning Procedures and Layouts 231

Tips for Cooking with Glucose in Mind 237

Selection of Low-Glycemic Fixtures 243

Alternatives that Work for Sugar and High-Carb Fixings 249

Top 5 Hacks to reduce Blood Sugar Increase 255

Cooking Techniques for Glucose Management
.... 259

Control of Segments and Dinner Planning 265

Equipment and Devices for Glucose-Compatible Cooking 272

FAQs 278

CONCLUSION 292

INTRODUCTION

We're glad you're here, "The Glucose Goddess Cookbook"! This cookbook aims to inspire people who want to live a balanced and meaningful life while controlling their blood sugar levels. This book is here to support you on your path, whether you have been given a diabetes diagnosis, you have been classified as pre-diabetic, or you are just looking to switch to a healthier eating pattern.

For making ordinary components into spectacular culinary masterpieces, Michelle has a rare talent. She was determined to impart her expertise to the world since she had a natural understanding of the complex connection between nutrition and health.

Michelle set out on a quest to write a cookbook that would transform the way people thought about their health. She was motivated by her own experience learning the importance of diet in controlling blood sugar levels. In her ideal world, people would be able to enjoy every bite without compromising their health. Delicious meals and glycemic management would coexist peacefully.

Michelle's fervor, knowledge, and steadfast commitment gave rise to The Glucose Goddess Cookbook. By leading readers on a transforming journey in the direction of balance and energy, it came to be seen as a testament to the blending of culinary talent with scientific understanding.

It wasn't merely a compilation of recipes in Michelle's cookbook. It served as a beacon, showing the way to a healthier and more fulfilling existence. She packed its pages with tantalizing breakfast treats, filling lunches, delectable dinners, and seductive desserts — all expertly prepared to control blood sugar levels without sacrificing flavor.

However, Michelle's book covered more than just cooking. It gave an in-depth analysis of glucose and its effects on health. It offered helpful hints for controlling blood glucose levels, navigating shopping stores, and understanding nutrition labels. By giving people the information and resources they need, it enabled them to take control of their own health.

People from all walks of life embraced the wisdom of the Glucose Goddess Cookbook as word of it travelled throughout the nation. The act of nourishing one's body and mind brought families together to cook, friends to congregate at the table, and newfound delight to the people who did it.

"The Glucose Goddess Cookbook" includes a holistic approach to health and wellness, not just a focus on what you eat. In this lesson, the significance of embracing balance in all facets of life—from diet to exercise to stress reduction—will be discussed. You can improve your overall quality of life and glucose control by implementing straightforward but effective lifestyle changes.

The Glucose Goddess Cookbook is your companion as you adopt a way of life that supports glucose regulation, encourages balanced nutrition, and recognizes the delight of delectable food. Each dish has been carefully designed to satisfy your glycemic targets while providing the most flavor and nutrition.

As a result, get ready to start a gastronomic journey that will change the way you eat and live. Let these pages' recipes motivate you to become the Glucose Goddess you were born to be.

The Glucose Goddess Cookbook's story serves as a constant reminder that we can change our life one delicious bite at a time by combining information, imagination, and a dash of culinary magic. Let the adventure begin, and may the Glucose Goddess Cookbook's influence motivate you to embrace the many rewards of a healthy, glucose-friendly lifestyle.

CHAPTER 1

What's Glucose Again?

The word "glucose" is a derivative of the Greek word for "sweet." Your body uses this particular type of sugar, which it obtains from the food you consume, as fuel. The term "blood glucose" or "glucose" refers to the substance that travels from your bloodstream to your phones.

Glucose from your blood is transferred into your cells by the molecule insulin for use as fuel and storage. Higher than usual levels of glucose are present in the blood of those who have diabetes. They may not respond to insulin as well as they should or may require more insulin to get the job done.

Your kidneys, eyes, and other organs can suffer damage from having high blood sugar levels for an extended period of time.

A basic source of energy for the body is glucose, a form of sugar. It is a type of simple carbohydrate that acts as the main source of energy for several biological functions. Because they are little, glucose molecules are quickly absorbed into the circulation after digestion.

During digestion, the carbohydrates in foods like bread, pasta, fruits, and vegetables are broken down into smaller molecules, which results in the production of glucose.

These carbs may take the form of starches, which are complex carbohydrates, or simple sugars like sucrose or fructose. No matter how they start, the body changes these carbohydrates into glucose to use as fuel.

After entering the bloodstream, glucose is distributed to all of the body's cells, where it provides energy for cellular processes. For organs and tissues that need a steady supply of energy, like the brain, muscles, and red blood cells, glucose is especially crucial.

The pancreas releases the hormone insulin in response to growing blood glucose levels to make sure that glucose is utilized by the cells effectively. The role of insulin is that it unlocks the cells, enabling glucose to enter and be used as energy. Glycogen, which is stored as excess glucose in the liver and muscles and released as needed when blood glucose levels fall, can be broken down and stored glucose.

Overall, glucose is essential for preserving the body's energy balance and supporting several physiological processes. It is a crucial part of a balanced diet and provides the body's cells with important fuel, enabling us to carry out everyday tasks and keep our health at its best.

How Your Body Produces Glucose

Bread, potatoes, and organic products are the main sources of it along with other carb-rich food items. Food travels through your stomach and gullet as you eat it. It is cut up into small pieces there by catalysts and acids. A glucose delivery is made during the contact.

When you swallow something, it goes into your digestive system. Your circulatory system receives it there and then. Insulin aids in the transport of glucose to your cells once it is in the circulation.

The Capacity for Energy

The level of glucose in your blood is meant to remain constant by your body. Every day, your pancreas' beta cells check your blood glucose levels. Following a meal, the beta cells release insulin into the bloodstream as soon as blood glucose levels rise. By acting as a key, insulin unlocks the cells of the liver, muscle, and fat, allowing glucose to enter.

Glucose, amino acids (the building blocks of protein), and lipids are used as energy sources by a substantial majority of your body's cells. The primary source of food for your brain, though, is this. In order to help them handle data, nerve cells and compound couriers there require it. Your brain wouldn't be able to perform admirably without it.

Your body stores excess glucose in the form of tiny containers called glycogen in the liver and muscles after using the necessary energy. Your body can store enough to keep you full for roughly a day.

Your blood sugar level falls after two hours without eating. It stops making insulin in your pancreas. The pancreas' alpha cells begin to produce glucagon, a different type of hormone.

The liver is prompted to remove, store, and convert glycogen back to glucose.

In order to replenish your supply until you are once again ready to eat, that motions to your circulatory system. Using a combination of side effects, amino acids, and lipids, your liver can also produce its own glucose.

Hyperglycemia and Diabetes

After eating, your blood glucose level usually rises. As insulin transports glucose into your cells, it then plummets a few hours later. Your glucose level should be under 100 mg/dl in the hours between meals. Your fasting glucose level is what we're talking about.

In diabetes, there are two types:

- You require extra insulin if you have type 1 diabetes. Where insulin is produced in the pancreas, the safe framework attacks and destroys cells.

- Cells respond to insulin improperly in type 2 diabetes. In order to get glucose into the cells, the pancreas must produce more and more insulin. The pancreas suffers long-term damage and is unable to produce enough insulin to treat the body's problems.

Glucose cannot enter cells if there is not enough insulin. The high amount of blood sugar persists. High blood sugar, often known as hyperglycemia, is defined as a level that is greater than 200 mg/dl two hours after a meal or greater than 125 mg/dl while fasting.

Vascular damage can occur to the vessels that carry oxygen-rich blood to your organs if there is an excess of glucose in your circulation system for an extended period of time. A high blood glucose level increases your risk of:

- Respiratory disease, stroke, and coronary artery disease
- A kidney infection
- Nerve damage
- Retinopathy is an eye condition.

Tests for glucose must be performed often in diabetics. Maintaining stable blood glucose levels and avoiding these entanglements can be helped by exercise, nutrition, and medication.

Supplies of Glucose

- **Diet:** When we eat carbohydrates like bread, rice, pasta, fruits, and vegetables, our bodies break them down into glucose.
- **Liver:** By releasing glucose that has been stored in the liver into circulation when needed, the liver is essential in managing blood glucose levels.
- **Blood glucose levels** are controlled.
- **The hormone insulin,** which aids in transferring glucose from the bloodstream into cells, is released by the pancreas when we eat carbs. Additionally, insulin makes it

easier for extra glucose to be stored as glycogen in the muscles and liver.

- **Glucagon:** When blood glucose levels are low, the pancreas secretes glucagon, a hormone that prompts the liver to re-convert glycogen that has been stored as glucose. This action raises blood glucose levels.

The Significance of Glucose to the Body

1. **Energy Production:** Glucose is the main source of energy for our cells, providing power for vital functions including muscular contractions, brain activity, and cellular metabolism.

2. **Glucose is essential for brain function** since the brain almost exclusively uses it for energy, which makes it essential for mental and cognitive function.

3. **Red Blood Cells:** Red blood cells, which carry oxygen throughout the body, only have glucose as a source of energy.

4. **Diabetes and Health:**
- **Blood Glucose Levels:** Overall health must keep blood glucose levels steady. Hyperglycemia, or high blood sugar levels, can result from diseases like diabetes, whereas hypoglycemia, or low blood sugar levels, can be brought on by some drugs or ailments like insulin overdose.

- The glycemic index (GI) classifies foods according to how quickly they elevate blood sugar levels. Blood glucose levels rise quickly in response to foods with a high GI, but more slowly and gradually in response to those with a low GI.

- **Diabetes:** Diabetes is a disease that results in abnormal glucose regulation and high blood glucose levels. It needs to be carefully managed by food decisions, medication, and lifestyle adjustments.

5. **Diabetes and Nutrition:**
- **Balanced carbohydrate intake:** A balanced diet should contain a variety of carbohydrates, including glucose. Choosing to consume complex carbs, such

as whole grains, legumes, and fiber-rich meals, helps promote stable blood glucose levels by delivering a continuous release of glucose into the bloodstream.

- **Portion control:** Keeping an eye on serving sizes and taking the overall makeup of meals into account will help control blood sugar levels and avert spikes and crashes.

- Making wise dietary decisions, controlling blood sugar levels, and enhancing general health all depend on having a solid understanding of glucose. An individual can assist their glucose metabolism and improve their well-being by eating carbohydrates in moderation and engaging in frequent physical activity.

Knowledge of Glucose and Health Effects

Our bodies' main source of energy is glucose, a form of sugar. It is essential for supplying energy to our cells, tissues, and organs. For those who are treating diabetes or trying to avoid blood sugar imbalances, however, maintaining stable glucose levels is crucial for overall health.

Our bodies convert the carbs we eat into glucose, which is then absorbed into the bloodstream. By boosting glucose's absorption into cells, where it may be utilized for energy, the pancreatic hormone insulin aids in glucose regulation. However, issues arise when the body either produces insufficient insulin (as in type 1 diabetes) or develops a resistance to insulin's effects (as in type 2 diabetes).

Numerous health problems might result from unchecked or persistently elevated glucose levels. Diabetes can contribute to long-term complications like cardiovascular disease, nerve damage, renal problems, and vision problems for people who have it. Fluctuations in blood glucose levels can have an impact on a person's overall health and well-being, even in those without diabetes.

Making wise food decisions requires an understanding of the effects of glucose on health. A useful tool for ranking foods high in carbohydrates and low in blood sugar levels is the Glycemic Index (GI). Blood sugar levels are quickly raised by foods with a high GI value, while they are gradually raised by foods with a low GI value.

The Glucose Goddess Cookbook places a strong emphasis on using low-glycemic foods in all of its recipes. These substances have a more gradual effect on blood glucose levels, reducing the likelihood of unexpected spikes and crashes. Choose whole meals that are strong in fiber, good fats, and lean proteins to help maintain stable blood sugar levels, improve satiety, and improve general health.

Additionally, we promote portion control and mindful eating. Effective glucose level management can be achieved by being aware of the quantity and quality of carbs consumed. Additionally, consuming foods high in proteins, lipids, and fiber can slow down the digestion and absorption of glucose, reducing the likelihood of sharp changes in blood sugar.

We may maintain stable glucose levels and take charge of our health by being aware of how glucose affects our body and making educated decisions. The Glucose Goddess Cookbook is here to help you along the way by providing scrumptious recipes and insightful advice to enable you to successfully live a lifestyle that is friendly to glucose. Accepting the power of knowledge, let's create decisions that promote our well-being!

Choosing to Live a Balanced and Glucose-Friendly Lifestyle

It takes more than merely following recipe instructions in a cookbook to embrace a balanced and glucose-friendly lifestyle. Assisting glucose regulation and general well-being, it entails forming healthy routines and making deliberate decisions. To adopt a balanced and glucose-friendly lifestyle, keep the following points in mind:

Exercise and physical activity should be done regularly to maintain a healthy weight, enhance insulin sensitivity, and control blood sugar levels. Make it a habit to include the activities you enjoy in your daily schedule.

Pay attention to your body's signals of hunger and fullness as you eat mindfully. Eat mindfully, take your time with each bite, and pay attention to your body's satiety cues. To concentrate on your food and make better choices, stay away from distractions like TV or screens while you're eating.

Keep Hydrated. Throughout the day, sip copious amounts of water to keep yourself hydrated. Digestion is aided, overall health is supported, and blood sugar levels can be regulated with water. Limit your intake of sugary drinks and replace them with water, herbal tea, or infused water.

Blood sugar levels can be impacted by chronic stress. Find appropriate coping mechanisms for stress, such as mindfulness exercises, relaxation techniques, meditation, or relaxing hobbies and pastimes.

Get Good Sleep. Try to get enough good sleep every night. Hormonal imbalances and blood sugar regulation can both be impacted by poor sleep. To support the best possible sleep, establish a regular sleep schedule and designate a sleep-friendly environment.

Maintaining Regular Blood Sugar Checks. As directed by your healthcare provider, maintain regular blood sugar checks. This aids in your understanding of how various diets and lifestyle choices affect your blood sugar levels and enables you to make the required modifications to your management strategy.

Seek Expert Advice. Speak with a Registered Dietitian or other Healthcare Professional with Experience in Diabetes or Glucose Management. They can help you develop a unique strategy for controlling your blood sugar levels and offer you customized advice and assistance with meal planning.

Social Support. Surround yourself with a network of loved ones and friends who support and understand your glucose-friendly way of life. Ask for their help in making healthy decisions and share your objectives and difficulties with them.

A balanced and glucose-friendly lifestyle requires a long-term commitment, so keep that in mind. It's about implementing long-lasting adjustments that will promote your health and well-being. You may successfully control your blood sugar levels and live a full and active life with perseverance, consistency, and the appropriate attitude.

Hacks on how to control Blood Sugar

For people with diabetes or those trying to keep their blood sugar levels stable, controlling glucose levels is essential. To assist you in effectively monitoring and regulating your blood sugar levels, consider the following advice:

Consume a diet that is well-balanced and rich in whole foods, such as fruits, vegetables, whole grains, lean proteins, and healthy fats. To reduce blood sugar spikes, include foods with a low glycemic index (GI).

Control your portion sizes to prevent consuming too many carbohydrates. For an accurate serving size estimate, use measuring cups, food scales, or visual cues. Your personal carbohydrate goals can be established by speaking with a trained dietician.

Choose complex carbohydrates. Go for complex carbohydrates, such as those found in whole grains, legumes, and vegetables. Since these foods are high in fiber, digestion and absorption of glucose are slowed down, causing blood sugar levels to rise more gradually.

Monitoring your intake of carbohydrates will help you determine how different foods will affect your blood sugar levels. You can accomplish this by keeping a meal diary, using a mobile app, or by utilizing a glucose monitor that has carbohydrate-counting capabilities.

Include lean proteins and healthy fats. Combining carbohydrates with these nutrients can aid in slowing down digestion and preventing sharp increases in blood sugar levels. Include sources of protein like poultry, fish, tofu, and lentils in your diet, along with good-for-you fats like avocado, almonds, and olive oil.

Regular exercise. Exercise regularly to help your body become more sensitive to insulin and better able to utilize glucose. Along with strength training activities, aim for at least 150 minutes per week of moderate-intensity aerobic activity.

Keep yourself hydrated by drinking lots of water all day long. A healthy blood flow is supported by proper hydration, which may also aid in controlling blood sugar.

Regular glucose checking. Use a glucose meter or continuous glucose monitoring equipment to check your blood sugar levels regularly. Having a better understanding of how various foods, activities, and lifestyle choices affect your blood glucose levels will help you make the necessary modifications.

Chronic stress might have an impact on glucose levels. To assist keep stress levels under control, incorporate stress management strategies like deep breathing exercises, meditation, or engaging in activities you like.

Consult with your healthcare team, which should include trained dietitians and doctors, for individualized advice and assistance in controlling your blood glucose levels. They can offer precise suggestions made specifically for your requirements.

Never forget that controlling your blood glucose levels is a dynamic process that calls for self-awareness, constancy, and frequent monitoring. You may take charge of your glucose levels, advance general health, and well-being, and work closely with your healthcare team by putting these suggestions into practice.

CHAPTER 2

Morning Delights

"Do you remember your mother telling you that breakfast is the important meal of the day?"

It turned out that she knew exactly what she was talking. The biggest meal of the day is undoubtedly breakfast.

You discover that you are lagging a few moments behind while the day is just getting started. You're running behind schedule and are preoccupied with a lot of things, save for a healthy meal, such as your hectic schedule, your next drive, and your next cup of coffee. However, it is worth repeating: An equitable eating schedule should include morning dinners because breakfast is the primary meal of the day. Learn why you should dedicate a few minutes to it each morning.

Fundamental Support. Having breakfast helps you start the day off well by providing your body with essential nutrients and minerals (fuel). Your body needs gasoline to function, much like a car. It's not necessary to grab an espresso and a donut for breakfast. A good breakfast should consist of a variety of foods, including whole grains, proteins like peanut butter, lean meat, chicken, fish, or eggs, yoghurt, parfaits, smoothies, and fresh or frozen agricultural products.

Boost in Energy. Consider this you've gone 13 hours without eating if you eat dinner at six o'clock in the evening and wake up at seven o'clock in the morning. If you skip breakfast, it will be 18 hours before you can eat again. When you skip meals for that long, your body is deprived of the food it needs to function properly.

Your body and brain are fueled by breakfast, which offers them the glucose they need to function properly and fight fatigue. If you skip breakfast, you'll noticeably have less energy throughout the day.

Strengthened Fixation. Having a substantial breakfast helps you stay alert and useful throughout the morning. Fixation, inventiveness, coordination, and critical thinking all grow more as a result. You have greater energy after breakfast, so you can be more truly active.

A happier frame of mind. You will typically be cranky and irritable when you are eager. Your body needs fuel, thus it is currently operating on void. Your entire framework is affected by this. Who needs to hang out with someone like you? Every day, have breakfast to help yourself and those around you.

Time spent with the family. The best time to have a meal with your loved ones is over breakfast with your family. It's a remarkable way of outlining the predisposition for sharing an equal feast as well. When you eat breakfast every day, you are likely to consume a better diet generally, which creates the foundation for a better life.

A wholesome way to start the day is with breakfast. Breakfast is the foundation of a healthy eating regimen and refuels your body while also improving your mood, sharpening your focus, helping you maintain a healthy weight. A good breakfast can be quickly prepared and easily consumed, providing benefits that endure throughout the entire day.

Here are a few scrumptious breakfast recipes that are low in sugar:

Smoothie with Vanilla Protein

This protein-rich vanilla smoothie has a subtle fruit flavor and is creamy. It makes for the ideal nutritious breakfast or post-workout snack.

Are you looking for a protein-rich snack to enjoy? Try this Vanilla Protein Smoothie instead! It has 25% of your daily protein requirements and is bursting with creamy, gently fruity flavor. Even better: the ingredients are all-natural and tasty and contain no protein powder! It is a favorite of our 3-year-old and tastes more like a vanilla milkshake than a protein drink, which made it popular in our household. You've already consumed half of your recommended daily protein if you take the large portion. It's the ideal post-workout snack, breakfast smoothie, or energy smoothie.

Why this protein shake is the best.

Protein shakes occasionally taste like healthy food or have an artificial protein powder aftertaste. That's exactly the opposite of this. Why would you make a protein smoothie?

- It tastes pure and delicious. It tastes like tropical fruit mixed with a vanilla milkshake.
- Its texture is incredibly smooth and creamy. The ideal thickness for drinking!
- It contains several nutritious nutrients. There is only fruit and yogurt; no extra sweetness is used.
- Without using protein powder, it is protein-rich. It is packed with organic sources of protein, including Greek yogurt and peanut butter.

What goes into a protein smoothie?

A protein smoothie containing 13 grams of protein can be made with this small list of ingredients. 25% of your daily protein needs are met by it. What you'll need is as follows:

- **Greek yogurt:** Greek yogurt is a great source of high-quality protein. Probiotics are also included to improve intestinal health.

- Another source of protein is peanut butter. **Dependable peanut butter**. It gives this smoothie a rich flavor without becoming overbearing.

- **Frozen pineapple:** This smoothie's main ingredient, pineapple, adds the perfect amount of sweetness.

- **Banana:** The texture becomes creamier and adds additional delicious flavor.

- **Milk:** Combine everything in the blender with a small amount of milk as the liquid; use whichever kind you have on hand.
- **Vanilla:** The final flavor is provided by vanilla extract! Produces two smoothies or one very huge smoothie.

This recipe yields two small smoothies, each of which has 25% of the recommended daily protein intake. Or, if you'd like, you can increase the protein content even more and have the entire smoothie at once! One serving of the smoothie has a staggering 26 grams of protein. 50% of your daily demands are met by that.

Smoothie Container

Smoothies are best consumed right away. However, this protein shake only needs to be refrigerated for one to two days when kept in a sealed container or a mason jar with the top on it. It might split apart, which is quite normal. Simply give it a shake, and you're ready to go! Making breakfast the night before is a good way to have it ready in the morning.

Protein Smoothie Recipe

Duration: 5 minutes

Servings: 2

This recipe for a protein smoothie is gluten-free and vegetarian. This protein-rich vanilla smoothie has a subtle fruit flavor and is creamy. It makes for the ideal nutritious breakfast or post-workout snack.

Ingredients

- 1 cup of frozen pineapple is used.
- Banana, one, at room temperature
- 2/4 cup peanut butter
- Greek yogurt, ½ cup
- 12 cup milk (or oat, almond, or coconut milk)
- ½ tsp. vanilla extract

- 8 cubes of ice
- We used fresh raspberries and toasted coconut as a garnish.

Directions

Step 1: Blend all the ingredients while chopping up the bananas. Until smooth, blend.

Step 2: Serve right away or keep in the fridge for two days in a sealed jar.

Tropical Smoothies

We reach for something cool and refreshing as the temperature rises on warm summer days. Enter fruity, creamy smoothies for the summer.

In addition to being simple to make, these blended drinks showcase the greatest fruit of the season in unique ways. Melting under the hot sun? You can make healthy smoothie recipes with these simple fresh ingredients that you may enjoy all year long.

With vibrant citrus, fresh strawberries, and juicy peaches, these recipes showcase the best of summer's flavors. Want to consume more greens? Fruit may command attention, but unseen vegetables also shine: Smoothies made of sweet mango and carrot combine beautifully, while smoothies made of bananas and honey receive a nutritional boost from spinach. By turning these slurpable drinks into smoothie bowls, you can change your daily routine!

A sour raspberry smoothie with Greek yogurt becomes a thick, creamy concoction that is ideal for topping with kiwi, coconut flakes, or chia seeds. What makes these summertime beverages so great? You can prepare them in less than 5 minutes, and they're quite easy to make, so you'll be lounging by the pool in no time.

Blend up one of these fruity drinks for a new go-to smoothie, whether you're looking for a more substantial summer drink recipe or a quick breakfast option. Choose your preferred recipe (or try them all), pour it into your favorite festive glass, and start relaxing in the sunshine!

Servings: 2
Duration: 5 minutes

Ingredients
For Mango Madness
- Orange juice, 1 cup
- Coconut yogurt, half a cup
- 1.25 cups of frozen mango

- 1 medium carrot, grated coarsely

Truffle Ingredients

- ½ cup each of coconut yogurt and water
- Strawberries, one cup
- Frozen peaches, half a cup

Leafy Goddess Ingredients

- Unsweetened almond milk in a half-cup
- Honey yogurt, half a cup
- Two bananas, frozen after being sliced up.
- Baby spinach, 3 cups

Razzle-Dazzle

- Low-fat milk, ½ cup
- Nonfat Greek yogurt, half a cup
- Frozen raspberries, 2 cups
- Two bananas, peeled and chopped

Directions

Step 1: Blend the items in a blender until completely smooth.

Step 2: Create a smoothie bowl. Make a bowl of Razzle-Dazzle Smoothie and serve. Add raspberries, coconut flakes, and kiwi slices on top.

Blueberry Smoothie Bowl

Servings: 2
Time Total: 10 minutes

Ingredients

- Frozen blueberries, one cup
- Unsweetened almond milk in a half-cup
- Protein powder, 1 ½ scoops
- Unsweetened almond butter, 2 tablespoons
- Pure vanilla extract, 1 teaspoon
- Fresh blueberries, half a cup
- Vanilla granola, ¼ cup
- Sliced almonds, 2 tablespoons
- 2 teaspoons hemp seeds
- The ground cinnamon, 1 teaspoon

Directions

Step 1: Blend almond milk, protein powder, almond butter, and vanilla in a blender until smooth. Distribute across two bowls.

Step 2: Before serving, garnish each bowl with fresh blueberries, granola, almonds, hemp seeds, and cinnamon.

Mocha Banana Smoothie

Time Total: 5 minutes
Servings: 2

The ideal post-workout snack, dessert, or breakfast is this banana mocha smoothie.

This smoothie is simple to make, incredibly creamy, and delicious! The combo of banana, chocolate, and coffee is unbeatable. How can that trio be in trouble? Oh! Don't press me on the additions of cinnamon and cardamom. They add a distinctive touch to this smoothie. Do you intend to serve this for dessert, a snack, or breakfast? For all of the aforementioned, it works!

How to Smoothie up this Protein

All ingredients should be added to a powerful blender and blended on high for one minute, or until thoroughly incorporated. If the smoothie is too thick, add more almond milk. The consistency of the protein powder you use will determine this.

Dragon Fruit Smoothie

The only five items required to make a dragon fruit smoothie. It can be made in 2 minutes, has a lovely magenta color, and is a delicious delight for the palate.

Time Total: 5 Minutes
Servings: 2

Ingredients

- 1 cup dragon fruit, either fresh or frozen
- Two bananas, fresh or frozen
- 12 cups frozen cauliflower florets
- 2 tablespoons of protein powder in vanilla
- 1 ½ cups of your preferred milk

Directions

Step 1: Blend all of the ingredients in a high-speed blender for 60 to 120 seconds, or until the mixture is smooth and creamy.

Step 2: If the smoothie is too thick or too sugary for you, taste it and add extra milk or sweetener as needed.

Step 3: Put the mixture in a cup or Mason jar. Consume cold right away or keep in the refrigerator for up to 24 hours.

Omelette Packed With Protein

Duration: 10 Minutes
Time Total: 10 minutes
Servings: 1

This super food-rich, nutrient-dense, vitamin-rich omelet with high protein content will offer you the healthy start to your day that you deserve. The diversity of vegetables offers a ton of flavor and a wonderful balance to the egg's mild, creamy texture.

Ingredients
- Two huge eggs
- ¼ cups of bell peppers, diced
- tomato dice, one-fourth cup
- 2 tablespoons of onions, diced
- (Optional) ¼ cup low-fat cheese crumbles
- Pepper and salt as desired
- For garnish, use fresh herbs like parsley or chives.

Directions

Step 1: Whisk the eggs, salt, and pepper in a bowl.

Step 2: Cooking spray is lightly applied to a non-stick skillet before heating it over medium heat.

Step 3: To the skillet, add the diced bell peppers, tomatoes, and onions. They should be mildly softened after a few minutes of sautéing.

Step 4: Over the sautéed vegetables, pour the whisked eggs. Cook until the bottom is set, just a few minutes.

Step 5: Half of the omelet should have cheese sprinkled on top of it (if using). Overlap the remaining piece with the cheese.

Step 6: Cook for one more minute, or until the eggs are done and the cheese is melted.

Step 7: Serve hot and garnish with fresh herbs.

Quinoa Breakfast Bake

Ingredients

- 1 cup cooked quinoa and 1 cup chopped spinach
- ¼ cups of bell peppers, diced

- Onions, diced, ¼ cup
- Two huge eggs
- ¼ cups of low-fat cheese, shredded
- Pepper and salt as desired

Directions

Step 1: Set the oven's temperature to 350°F (175°C). Grease a baking pan very lightly.

Step 2: Combine the cooked quinoa, chopped spinach, diced bell peppers, and diced onions in a sizable bowl. To distribute the ingredients equally, thoroughly mix.

Step 3: Beat the eggs in another bowl. Over the quinoa mixture, add the beaten eggs, and toss until everything is thoroughly coated.

Step 4: Mix the ingredients once more before adding the low-fat cheese. To taste, add salt and pepper to the food.

Step 5: Spread out the quinoa mixture equally in the baking dish after transferring it there.

Step 6: Bake for 20 to 25 minutes in a preheated oven, or until the top is golden brown and the edges are just beginning to crisp up.

Step 7: Before serving, take it out of the oven and allow it to cool for a while.

Step 8: As a wholesome and satisfying breakfast choice, cut into squares and serve hot.

This quinoa breakfast bake is a filling, protein-rich dish that will keep you full all morning.

Quinoa, spinach, bell peppers, and onions work together to offer a variety of nutrients; eggs and cheese contribute protein and a delectable flavor. Feel free to alter the recipe to suit your tastes by including other vegetables or herbs. It can be prepared in advance and warmed up for a quick and practical breakfast choice. Enjoy!

Pancakes with Berry Compote and No Gluten

Ingredient

- 1 cup mixed gluten-free flour

- 1 tablespoon sugar (or other preferred sweetener)
- One tablespoon of baking powder
- A half-teaspoon of baking soda
- ¼ teaspoons of salt
- Buttermilk (or a dairy-free substitute) in one cup
- One big egg
- 2 tablespoons of melted butter (or a substitute made without dairy)
- Vanilla extract, 1 teaspoon

Berry Compote ingredients include:
- 1 cup of mixed berries, including raspberries, blueberries, and strawberries
- 2 tablespoons sugar (or other preferred sweetener)
- One teaspoon of lemon juice

- (Optional) ½ teaspoon corn flour for thickening

Directions for making pancakes:

Step 1: Mix the sugar, salt, baking soda, baking powder, and gluten-free flour in a big basin.

Step 2: Combine the buttermilk, egg, melted butter, and vanilla extract in a separate basin.

Step 3: After adding the liquid components, mix the dry ingredients only until they are barely blended. Avoid over-mixing; a few lumps are acceptable.

Step 4: A nonstick griddle or skillet should be heated to medium. Use butter or cooking spray to lightly grease.

Step 5: For each pancake, pour 1/4 cup of the batter into the skillet. Cook until surface bubbles appear, flip, and cook for an additional 1 to 2 minutes, or until golden brown.

Step 6: While you make the berry compote, transfer the cooked pancakes to a platter and cover with a clean kitchen towel to keep them warm.

How to make berry compote:

Step 1: Mix the mixed berries, sugar, and lemon juice in a small pot. Cook the berries, occasionally tossing, over medium heat until they begin to break down and release juices.

Step 2: If preferred, make a slurry out of the corn flour and a tablespoon of water before adding it to the saucepan. To blend, thoroughly stir.

Step 3: The compote should be cooked for a further 2 to 3 minutes to achieve a minor thickening.

Step 4: Take it off the fire and give it a few minutes to cool.

Step 5: To serve, arrange the gluten-free pancakes in a stack on a platter and top them with the warm berry compote. For even more decadence, you can top it with a dollop of whipped cream or a dusting of powdered sugar.

As a pleasant breakfast treat, savor these fluffy and delectable gluten-free pancakes with a burst of fruity sweetness from the berry compote.

Fresh Fruit and Chia Seed Pudding

Ingredients
- Chia seeds, ¼ cup
- 1 cup almond milk without sugar (or any other milk of your choosing)

- 1 tablespoon honey (or other preferred sweetener
- One-half teaspoon of vanilla extract
- A variety of fresh fruits (such as diced mangoes, sliced bananas, or sliced berries)
- Granola, coconut flakes, or nuts are optional toppings.

Directions

Step 1: Chia seeds, almond milk, honey, and vanilla extract should all be combined in a bowl. Stir thoroughly to distribute the chia seeds evenly.

Step 2: Give the mixture another toss after letting it sit for about 5 minutes. This will stop the chia seeds from clumping.

Step 3: Allow the chia seeds to absorb the liquid and take on the consistency of custard by covering the bowl and placing it in the refrigerator for at least two hours or overnight. To keep the seeds from sinking to the bottom during refrigeration, stir once or twice.

Step 4: Give the chia seed mixture one last stir once it has solidified to separate any remaining clumps. Put the chia seed pudding into dishes or jars to serve.

Step 5: Add a choice of fresh fruit toppings to each serving, such as chopped mangoes, sliced bananas, or sliced berries. For extra texture and flavor, top with optional ingredients like nuts, coconut flakes, or granola.

Chia seed pudding is velvety and filling, and the fresh fruits add a burst of freshness when served chilled.

A nutritious and adaptable breakfast option, chia seed pudding may be personalized with your preferred fruits and toppings. It has a wealth of minerals, including fiber and omega-3 fatty acids.

This dish offers a delectable way to savor chia seeds and get your day off to a cool start. To suit your taste preferences, feel free to experiment with various fruit and topping combinations.

CHAPTER 3

Scrumptious Lunch Meals

I have witnessed a lot of people vow not to eat their lunch, whether they are college students rushing to class, people trying to lose weight, or business professionals trying to get through mountains of desk work (only to acquire much more of them). This is a vice to develop, despite everything.

The important meal of the day is lunch.

You gain energy through eating. Midway through the afternoon, after lunch, your blood sugar levels rise, giving you the ability to focus until the end of the day.

-It has been proven that those who skip lunch will frequently gain more weight because they overeat at dinner to make up for it.

-While dining together, you can get to know others.

-Lunch is much more significant for children because it is when they obtain their afternoon nutrients and supplements, therefore it is much more important for them. Their real and psychological growth could be hampered if they don't receive the improvements their bodies require.

People rarely take pauses in the fast-paced world we live in today, yet taking a break is not a pointless endeavor. For one to be effective and to be healthy, they are essential.

Here are Glucose Goddess Cookbook's lunchtime meals:

Mediterranean Quinoa Salad

Ingredients
- Half a cup of cooked quinoa and a cup of cherry tomatoes make up this salad.
- Sliced cucumber, half a cup
- ¼ cup finely sliced red onion
- Kalamata olives, pitted and cut in half, ¼ cup

- ¼ cup feta cheese crumbles
- Two teaspoons of lemon juice, fresh
- Olive oil, extra virgin, two tablespoons
- 1 tablespoon freshly chopped parsley
- Pepper and salt as desired

Directions

Step 1: The cooked quinoa, Kalamata olives, feta cheese, cherry tomatoes, cucumber, and red onion should all be combined in a big bowl.

Step 2: Combine the lemon juice, parsley, olive oil, salt, and pepper in a small bowl.

Step 3: Toss the quinoa mixture with the dressing after pouring it over it.

Step 4: If necessary, adjust the seasoning.

Step 5: For a light and healthful lunch, serve the Mediterranean quinoa salad refrigerated or at room temperature.

Wrap with Avocado and Grilled Chicken

Ingredients

- 2 substantial whole-wheat tortillas
- 2 sliced grilled chicken breasts and 1 sliced ripe avocado
- Mixed salad greens, half a cup
- 2 teaspoons of sour cream or Greek yogurt

- A teaspoon of lime juice
- Pepper and salt as desired

Directions

Step 1: To prepare the dressing, blend the Greek yogurt or sour cream with the lime juice, salt, and pepper in a small bowl.

Step 2

Spread the dressing equally across each tortilla as you lay them out flat.

Step 3: Between the two tortillas, distribute the grilled chicken, avocado, and mixed salad leaves in slices.

Step 4: The tortillas should be securely rolled, tucking in the sides as you go.

Step 5: Cut the wrappers in half diagonally, and if required, fasten them with toothpicks.

Step 6: Enjoy the satisfying lunch option of grilled chicken and avocado wraps, which are delicious and high in protein.

Bell Peppers Stuffed with Quinoa
Ingredients
- 4 big, multicolored bell peppers
- Cooked quinoa, 1 cup

- ½ cup of rinsed and drained black beans
- A half-cup of corn kernels
- ¼ cup red onion, chopped
- Tomato dice, one-fourth cup
- ¼ cups of low-fat cheese, shredded
- 1 tablespoon freshly chopped cilantro
- 1 teaspoon of cumin, ground
- 50 ml of chili powder
- Pepper and salt as desired

Directions

Step 1: Set the oven's temperature to 375°F (190°C).

Step 2: The bell peppers' tops should be cut off so that the seeds and membranes can be removed.

Step 3: Combine the cooked quinoa, black beans, corn, tomatoes, red onion, cheese, chopped cilantro, cumin, chili powder, salt, and pepper in a big bowl.

Step 4: Put the quinoa mixture inside the bell peppers, carefully pressing it down so that it fills each one evenly.

Step 5: Bake the stuffed bell peppers for 25 to 30 minutes, or until the peppers are soft and the mixture is well cooked.

Step 6: Before serving, take them out of the oven and allow them to cool somewhat.

Step 7: Enjoy the quinoa-stuffed bell peppers as a healthy lunch alternative. They are tasty and filling.

Rice with Fried Cauliflower

Ingredients

- One tiny head of cauliflower
- Olive oil, 1 tbsp.
- Carrots, diced, in a cup
- ½ cup bell peppers, diced
- 50 g of frozen peas

- 2 minced garlic cloves
- 2 tablespoons of tamari (or low-sodium soy sauce for gluten-free options)
- One teaspoon of sesame oil
- 2 sliced green onions

Optional garnishes: Cilantro and sesame seeds, chopped

Directions

Step 1: Cauliflower should be cut into florets and placed in a food processor. Cauliflower should be pulsed until it resembles rice grains. Alternatively, you might use a box grater to grind the cauliflower.

Step 2: In a sizable skillet or wok set over medium heat, warm the olive oil.

Step 3: The skillet should now contain the diced carrots, bell peppers, and frozen peas. Stir-fry the vegetables for 3 to 4 minutes, or until they start to soften.

Step 4: When aromatic, stir-fry the minced garlic for 30 more seconds in the skillet.

Step 5: Place the cauliflower rice on the other side of the skillet after pushing the vegetables to one side. The cauliflower rice should be stir-fried for 3–4 minutes or until it is soft.

Step 6: In a skillet, combine the cauliflower rice and veggies. Pour the sesame oil and low-sodium soy sauce over the mixture. To evenly coat everything, thoroughly stir.

Step 7: Allow the flavors to merge by cooking for an additional 2 to 3 minutes.

Step 8: Remove from heat and, if like, garnish with sesame seeds, chopped cilantro, and thinly sliced green onions.

As a low-carb and healthier alternative to conventional fried rice, serve the cauliflower fried rice hot.

With cauliflower in place of typical rice, cauliflower fried rice reduces the amount of carbohydrates while maintaining a satisfying flavor and texture. It may be made with your preferred vegetables and protein sources and is a fantastic way to include more vegetables in your meal. Take pleasure in this healthier version of fried rice that will satisfy and nourish you.

Chickpea and Vegetable Stew

Ingredients

- Olive oil, 1 tbsp.
- 1 chopped onion, 2 minced garlic cloves, 1 diced carrot, 1 diced celery stalk, 1 diced bell pepper, 1 diced zucchini, and 1 can (1/4 oz.) shredded tomatoes
- Two cups of vegetable stock
- 1 can (15 oz.) washed and drained chickpeas
- One tablespoon of dried thyme

- 1 teaspoon of cumin, ground
- Paprika, half a teaspoon
- Pepper and salt as desired
- Chopped fresh parsley (for decoration)

Directions

Step 1: Over medium heat, warm the olive oil in a big pot.

To the pot, add the minced garlic and onion, and sauté until the garlic is aromatic and the onion is transparent.

Step 2: To the pot, add the diced zucchini, bell pepper, carrot, and celery. Vegetables should be sautéed for 5-7 minutes until they begin to soften.

Step 3: Add the vegetable broth and the diced tomatoes with their juice. To blend, thoroughly stir.

Step 4: To the pot, add the rinsed and drained chickpeas, dried thyme, cumin, paprika, salt, and pepper. The stew needs to be stirred to incorporate the spices.

Step 5: After bringing the mixture to a simmer, lower the heat. For 20 to 25 minutes, boil the stew with the lid on to let the flavors combine and the veggies soften.

Step 6: If necessary, add additional salt and pepper after tasting the stew.

Step 7: Hot chickpea and vegetable stew should be served with fresh parsley that has been chopped.

This filling stew of chickpeas, vegetables, and spices is bursting with fiber and plant-based protein. It makes a hearty and cozy lunch or dinner choice. Chickpeas and a range of vegetables together offer a healthy nutritional balance. You are welcome to alter the stew by including your preferred herbs, spices, or more veggies. Enjoy this tasty and filling lunch!

Sweet Potato Stuffed with Spinach and Feta

Ingredients

- 2 Substantial sweet potatoes
- Olive oil, 1 tbsp.
- Fresh spinach greens, 2 cups
- 2 minced garlic cloves
- ¼ cup feta cheese crumbles
- Pepper and salt as desired

Optional garnishes: Lemon wedges, fresh parsley chopped

Directions

Step 1: Set the oven's temperature to 400°F (200°C).

Step 2: Clean the sweet potatoes, then use a paper towel to wipe them dry. Use a fork to make a few fork pricks in the sweet potatoes.

Step 3: Put the sweet potatoes on a baking sheet that has been coated with aluminum foil or parchment paper. Bake the sweet potatoes for 40 to 50 minutes, or until they are soft to the touch.

Step 4: Melt the butter in a skillet over medium heat while the sweet potatoes are baking.

Step 5: When aromatic, add the minced garlic to the skillet and cook for 1-2 minutes.

Step 6: To the skillet, add the fresh spinach leaves, and cook until they are wilted.

Step 7: Turn off the heat and allow the spinach to gradually cool.

When the sweet potatoes are done cooking, take them out of the oven and let them cool until they are convenient to handle.

Step 8: Each sweet potato should have a pocket for the filling created by a lengthwise cut down the middle. Scoop off some of the sweet potato's inside flesh, leaving a border all the way around.

Step 9: In a bowl, mash the flesh that has been removed from the sweet potato and combine it with the sautéed spinach, garlic powder, and feta cheese. To taste, add salt and pepper to the food.

Step 10: Divide the spinach and feta mixture evenly between the two sweet potato pockets before spooning it in.

Step 11: Reheat the stuffed sweet potatoes in the oven for a further 5 to 10 minutes, or until the filling is thoroughly heated and the feta cheese is just beginning to melt.
After taking them out of the oven, give them some time to cool.

Sweet potatoes stuffed with spinach and feta are served with optional garnishes like lemon wedges and fresh parsley that has been cut.

A filling and healthy lunch alternative is this sweet potato with spinach and feta stuffing. Sweet potatoes, sautéed spinach, and tangy feta cheese come together to make a tasty and warming dish.

It's a terrific option for a nutritious lunch or dinner because it's high in vitamins, minerals, and fiber. Enjoy this nutritious and delectable lunch!

CHAPTER 4

Dinner Cuisine

Plan your dinner so that you can have a restful evening!

In many homes, supper is a crucial meal. If you eat quick meals for breakfast and lunch and are otherwise busy during the day, supper can be the mealtime that is most frequently associated with love and care.

I'm aware that this is where I exert the greatest effort. In many houses, supper is the main meal of the day and is therefore quite important because the whole family sits down to eat it.

Every bit as important as what you eat is the time you eat dinner. People frequently struggle with poor sleep quality, disturbed thinking, and strange nightmares after eating dinner extremely late.

Keep in mind that as the night draws closer, your ability to absorb nutrients weakens. Your dinner will feel lighter on your body the closer it is to nightfall. The best approach to stay light, sound, and get amazing sleep is to eat dinner before seven and go to bed within a couple hours of that time.

After a satisfying meal, when you get a good night's sleep, you can be sure that you'll make the greatest choices for each dinner the next day. This cycle of eating and sleeping is so intricately interwoven that even one specific meditation in any location has the power to spread a favourable influence elsewhere.

According to studies, consuming bitter greens supports the health of your liver. A fantastic way to feel more in control is to plan dinner for specific mixed greens. You can also have better sleep thanks to the magnesium in mixed greens.

Lighter dinners may be preferable, but a cup of soup may not be sufficient for everyone. If you have high pressure and an uneven distribution of glucose, you could travel quickly and condense your food quickly. You might want a nutritious dinner, such pan-seared sprouts, carrots, broccoli, and bok choy with some dark rice. It can be made more substantial and filling by adding some fish, providing you consume animal proteins.

Dinner may be a crucial meal if you struggle with painful fiery conditions because it will help you stay relaxed as the night goes on. Food selections with calming ingredients can help your body reduce chronic irritability and are wonderful!

Throughout the winter months, a hearty soup is a good idea. It can be helpful to eat soups that are delicious, healthful, and filling on their own. For a stock that includes onions, ginger, turmeric, coriander, and yellow pumpkin, green lentils or masoor can serve as an excellent foundation. Particularly when combined with black pepper and ginger, turmeric has a powerful soothing effect. Ginger is naturally anti-fitful and suppresses chemicals that cause aggravation and enlargement.

If you struggle with pressure and unease, every meal of the day is crucial to how you get through it. Various dietary options are ideal for calming unease and supporting the sensory system. Your synapses, such as those for serotonin and dopamine, are significantly impacted by these dietary sources. Adapt genic ingredients can be quite helpful for reducing stress and allowing your body to recover from anxiety and stress.

Shiitake mushrooms include potent phytonutrients that increase your capacity for flexibility. Combine them with natural tofu, which has a good amount of tryptophan for amazing sleep, sesame seeds, snow peas, mung beans, and some rice or buckwheat noodles.

Replace tofu with another excellent source of protein if you have chemical imbalances and can't handle it.

For the correct amount of phytonutrients, combine rice with colorful veggies. If you typically eat rice for dinner, combine it with a lot of lovely veggies to ensure a wide range of phytonutrients. Fresh green veggies are excellent for lymphatic development, vasodilation, and circulatory health. They act as a prebiotic and stimulate processing, and they also contain mitigating substances.

To stay warm during this chilly season, combine them with a variety of flavors, such as ginger. Garlic may energize a functioning brain and worry-free rest, so if you really do have trouble sleeping, keep some at dinner. Even though dinner is a substantial feast, there are many amazing culinary options to explore.

A good night's sleep, wise choices at breakfast and lunch, less irritability, more notable push-ability, improved processing, steady glucose, and less anxiety are all related to having a good dinner.

From the Glucose Goddess Cookbook, You wouldn't want to miss out these delicious dinner recipes:

Coconut Milk with Ginger and Sweet Potatoes Stew made with Kale and Lentils

The stew with ginger, sweet potatoes, and coconut milk is gorgeous, delicious, and very filling thanks to the kale and lentils. Quick recipe for a vegan meal!

Time Spent Prepping: 20 Minutes
Cooking Time: 45 Minutes
Total Time: 50 Minutes
Servings: 6

Ingredients

- One tablespoon of coconut oil
- A single medium yellow onion, diced
- 1–2 teaspoons of dried chili flakes
- ½ tsp. of coriander seeds
- ½ tsp. of cumin seeds
- Half a teaspoon of ground turmeric
- Fresh ginger, peeled and chopped, measuring 2 inches
- 3 minced garlic cloves

- 3 teaspoons each of sea salt, and freshly ground black pepper
- Peeled and sliced into 1-inch chunks of sweet potatoes weighing 1 ½ pounds (690 grams).
- Over 4 cups of vegetable stock and a half cup of brown lentils
- 13.5 oz. (400 ml) Can coconut milk with cream be
- 1 small bundle of chopped kale, with the stems removed (approximately 4 cups total).
- Chopped cilantro, more chili flakes, lime wedges, and nigella seeds are used as garnish.

Directions

Step 1: Over medium intensity, warm coconut oil in a large stockpot or Dutch oven. When the mixture is heated, add the onions and stir; simmer for 5 minutes, or until mellowed.

Step 2: Coriander, cumin, turmeric, red pepper chips, and other ingredients should be added at this point. Mix thoroughly and simmer for 30 seconds, stirring continuously, or until aromatic.

Step 3: For an additional 30 to 60 seconds, stir in the ginger and garlic.

Step 4: When adding the yams and lentils, stir in the flavoring thoroughly. Add salt and pepper for seasoning.

Step 5: By scraping up any sautéed bits on the bottom of the pot, add the vegetable stock and stir. Boiling water will be produced when the pot's top is placed on top of it. Reduce the heat to low while the pot is bubbling, and then slightly tilt the lid to let some of the heat escape.

Step 6: Cook the yams for around 25 to 30 minutes, until they are tender.

Step 7: Combine the greens with the coconut milk in the pot. A cover should be placed on top, and the stew should continue to simmer for around 3 minutes or until the kale is shriveled and a brilliant green color.

Step 8: Add cilantro and pepitas before serving hot.

Notes

Naturally sweet foods include coconut milk and sweet potatoes. To balance things out, I like to start with a lot of dried chili, but you should add however much you feel comfortable with.

It would be excellent to substitute chard or mustard greens for the kale.

Chicken Parmesan Baked

Preparation Time: 10 Minutes
Duration: 20 Minutes for Cooking
Servings: 4

Ingredients

- 2 skinless, boneless chicken breasts
- Whole wheat breadcrumbs in a cup
- Grated Parmesan cheese, ¼ cup
- A quarter-teaspoon dried basil
- Oregano, dry, 1/8 teaspoon
- A quarter-teaspoon of garlic powder
- Pepper and salt as desired
- One-fourth cup of marinara sauce
- Shredded mozzarella cheese, ¼ cup
- Sprigs of fresh basil, for decoration

Directions

Step 1: Set the oven's temperature to 400°F (200°C).

Step 2: The whole wheat bread crumbs, grated Parmesan cheese, dried basil, dried oregano, garlic powder, salt, and pepper should all be combined in a shallow dish.

Step 3: Each chicken breast should be dipped into the mixture of breadcrumbs and softly pressed to help the crumbs stick to the chicken.

Step 4: On a parchment-lined baking sheet, put the breaded chicken breasts.

Step 5: Bake the chicken for 20 minutes, or until it is thoroughly cooked and the crust is golden.

Step 6: After taking the chicken out of the oven, cover each breast with marinara sauce.
Over the sauce, scatter some mozzarella cheese.

Step 7: Once more, roast the chicken in the oven for 5 more minutes, or until the cheese is melted and bubbling.

Step 8: Fresh basil leaves are a nice garnish.
For a filling and complete dinner, serve the baked chicken parmesan with a side of steamed vegetables or a green salad.

Tofu and Vegetable Stir-Fry

Ingredients

- One tablespoon of sesame oil is a component.
- 1 cubed block of tofu
- Broccoli florets in a cup
- 1 sliced red bell pepper
- 1 julienned carrot
- Snap peas, 1 cup

- 2 minced garlic cloves
- Low-sodium soy sauce, two tablespoons
- A teaspoon of rice vinegar
- 1 teaspoon of maple syrup or honey
- ¼ teaspoon ginger, grated

Optional garnishes: green onions, chopped sesame seeds

Directions

Step 1: In a sizable skillet or wok, warm the sesame oil over medium heat.

Step 2: Cubed tofu should be added to the skillet and cooked until golden brown all around. From the skillet, take out the tofu, and set it aside.

Step 3: Add the broccoli florets, red bell pepper slices, carrot and snap pea juliennes, and minced garlic to the same skillet. Vegetables should be stir-fried for 4-5 minutes until crisp-tender.

Salmon Baked with Dill and Lemon

Ingredients

- 2 fillets of salmon
- Olive oil, two tablespoons

- Two teaspoons of lemon juice, fresh
- 1 lemon's zest
- 2 teaspoons chopped fresh dill
- Pepper and salt as desired

Directions

Step 1: Set the oven's temperature to 400°F (200°C).

Step 2: Salmon fillets should be put on a baking pan covered with parchment paper.

Step 3: Mix the olive oil, lemon juice, lemon zest, fresh dill, salt, and pepper in a small bowl.

Step 4: Salmon fillets should be well covered with the lemon-dill mixture before being poured over them.

Step 5: For the flavors to meld, give the salmon 10 to 15 minutes to marinate.

Step 6: For the salmon to be cooked to your preferred doneness, bake it in the preheated oven for 12 to 15 minutes, or until it flakes easily with a fork.

Step 7: Before serving, take the salmon out of the oven and allow it to rest for a while.

Step 8: As a healthy and flavorful dinner option, serve the baked salmon with lemon and dill.

A wonderful and healthful lunch is produced by combining soft baked salmon with citrusy lemon and fragrant dill. This recipe is easy to make and highlights the salmon's natural flavors. For a dinner that is full of flavor and substance, serve it with either roasted vegetables or a crisp salad. Enjoy!

Turkey Meatballs with Zucchini Noodles

Serving: 4

Time Total: 30 Minutes

For the Turkey Meatballs' Ingredients:
- 1 pound of turkey, ground

- If desired, use gluten-free ½ cup breadcrumbs.
- Grated Parmesan cheese, ¼ cup
- ¼ cup fresh parsley, cut finely
- 1/4 cup onion, chopped finely.
- 2 minced garlic cloves
- One big egg
- Oregano, dry, 1 teaspoon
- A half-teaspoon of dried basil
- Pepper and salt as desired

Regarding the Zucchini Noodles:
- 4 small courgette
- Olive oil, two tablespoons
- 2 minced garlic cloves
- Pepper and salt as desired

Regarding the Tomato Sauce:

- 1 can (14 oz.) chopped-up tomatoes
- One tablespoon of dried basil
- Oregano, dry, 1 teaspoon
- One-half teaspoon of garlic powder
- Pepper and salt as desired

Directions

Step 1: A baking sheet should be lined with parchment paper and the oven should be preheated to 400°F (200°C).

Step 2: Ground turkey, breadcrumbs, grated Parmesan cheese, chopped parsley, chopped onion, minced garlic, egg, dried oregano, dried basil, salt, and pepper should all be combined in a big bowl. To thoroughly incorporate all ingredients, stir well.

Step 3: On the prepared baking sheet, form the mixture into meatballs that are 1 to 2 inches in diameter.

Step 4: The meatballs should be cooked through and golden brown on the outside after 20 to 25 minutes in the preheated oven.

Step 5: Prepare the zucchini noodles and bake the meatballs simultaneously. To make zucchini noodles, use a vegetable peeler or spiralizer. Place aside.

Step 6: Olive oil should be heated in a sizable skillet over medium heat. Add the minced garlic and cook until fragrant, about 1 minute.

Step 7: Zucchini noodles should be added to the skillet and cooked for two to three minutes, or until just softened. To taste, add salt and pepper to the food. Place aside.

Step 8: Crushed tomatoes, dried basil, dried oregano, garlic powder, salt, and pepper should all be combined in a separate saucepan. To allow the flavors to blend, simmer the sauce for 10 to 15 minutes over low heat.

Step 9: Add the cooked meatballs to the tomato sauce and let them simmer for an additional five minutes.

Step 10: Serve the tomato sauce on top of the turkey meatballs and zucchini noodles.

Step 11: Take pleasure in this tasty and nutritious dish as a filling dinner alternative.

With the addition of zucchini noodles, these turkey meatballs offer a lighter and healthier variation of a traditional favorite.

The zucchini noodles give the dish a light, low-carb element while the turkey meatballs are moist and flavorful.

A wonderful and wholesome supper is created by combining all the ingredients with homemade tomato sauce. Take pleasure in this guilt-free meal alternative!

Pizza with Cauliflower Crust

Ingredients

For the cauliflower crust, you'll need:

- ¼ cup grated Parmesan cheese, ¼ cup shredded mozzarella cheese, and 1 medium cauliflower head
- Oregano, dry, 1 teaspoon
- One-half teaspoon of garlic powder
- 1 big egg and ¼ teaspoon salt

Those pizza toppings are:
- 50 ml of tomato sauce
- 1 cup of mozzarella cheese, shredded

Various toppings of your choosing (such as chopped tomatoes, sliced olives, sliced bell peppers, and mushrooms).

Directions

Step 1: A baking sheet should be lined with parchment paper and the oven should be preheated to 425°F (220°C).

Step 2: Cauliflower should be cut into florets and put in a food processor. Pulse until the cauliflower resembles rice-like grains.

Step 3: Put the cauliflower "rice" in a microwave-safe bowl and heat it for 5 to 6 minutes on high, or until it is tender and cooked.

Step 4: After letting the cooked cauliflower cool for a short while, transfer it to a fresh dish towel or piece of cheesecloth. Squeeze the cauliflower to remove as much liquid as you can.

Step 5: Cauliflower that has been squeezed, grated Parmesan, shredded mozzarella, dried oregano, garlic powder, salt, and an egg should all be combined in a mixing dish. Mix items thoroughly until well combined.

Step 6: On the prepared baking sheet, spread the cauliflower mixture out and shape it into a thin, round crust. Aim for a ¼ inch thickness or less.

The cauliflower crust should bake for 15 to 20 minutes in a preheated oven or until golden brown and firm to the touch. After removing the crust from the oven, give it some time to cool.

Step 7: Leave a thin border around the borders and cover the cauliflower crust with tomato sauce equally.

Step 8: Add your preferred toppings, then top with shredded mozzarella cheese.

Step 9: When the cheese is melted and bubbling, put the pizza back in the oven for a further 10-15 minutes of baking.

Before slicing, take the pizza out of the oven and let it cool for a while.

Step 10: Pizza with a cauliflower crust should be served hot so that you may enjoy this tasty and healthy pizza option.

If you're looking for a pizza dish with a low-carb or gluten-free crust, try this one with cauliflower. You may choose the toppings to suit your tastes, and the cauliflower crust is crunchy and tasty. It's a terrific way to eat more vegetables while still enjoying pizza. Good appetite!

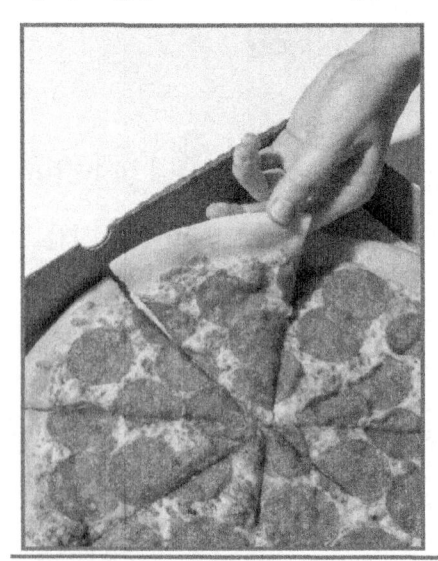

Roasted Chicken with Garlic and Herbs

Ingredients

- 4-5 pounds of one entire chicken
- 4 minced garlic cloves
- 2 teaspoons of chopped fresh rosemary
- 2 teaspoons of chopped fresh thyme
- 2 teaspoons of chopped fresh parsley
- Olive oil, two tablespoons
- 1 sliced lemon
- Pepper and salt as desired

Directions

Step 1: Set the oven's temperature to 425°F (220°C).

Step 2: Chicken should be rinsed and dried with paper towels.

Step 3: Olive oil, salt, pepper, minced garlic, chopped parsley, rosemary, and thyme should all be combined in a small bowl. For a paste, thoroughly combine.

Step 4: Make careful to cover the chicken's exterior as well as the area under the skin with the garlic and herb paste as you rub it in.

Step 5: Put the chicken in a baking or roasting pan.

Step 6: Place the cut lemon inside the chicken's cavity.

Step 7: To retain the shape of the chicken, tie the legs together with kitchen twine.

Step 8: The internal temperature of the chicken should reach 165°F (75°C) and the skin should be golden brown and crispy after roasting it in the preheated oven for an hour to an hour and 15 minutes.

Step 9: Before carving, take the chicken out of the oven and allow it to rest for 10 to 15 minutes.

Step 10: The chicken should be carved and served with your preferred side dishes, such as mashed potatoes or roasted veggies.

Step 11: Enjoy the tasty and filling roasted chicken with garlic and herbs as a dinner choice.

With a crispy golden skin and juicy, aromatic meat, this recipe for roasted chicken with garlic and herbs delivers. Lemon, fresh herbs, and garlic give the chicken a beautiful scent and improve its flavor. It's a traditional, hearty dish that goes well with anything. Enjoy!

Burgers with Portobello Mushrooms

Ingredients

- Portobello mushrooms, four, large
- Burger buns—four
- 4 cheese slices, optional
- 4 leaves of lettuce
- 4-slice tomatoes
- One finely sliced red onion

- 4 tablespoons of mayo
- Dijon mustard, two tablespoons
- Balsamic vinegar, two tablespoons
- Olive oil, two tablespoons
- Pepper and salt as desired

Directions

Step 1: Heat a grill pan or the grill to medium-high temperature.

Step 2: Remove the stems from the Portobello mushrooms and clean the caps with a moist towel.

Step 3: Mayonnaise, Dijon mustard, balsamic vinegar, olive oil, salt, and pepper should all be combined in a small bowl. The marinade for the mushrooms will be this.

Step 4: Make sure the marinade is thoroughly applied to the Portobello mushrooms on both sides.

Step 5: Place the mushrooms cap side down on the grill or grill pan. Cook the mushrooms for about 4-5 minutes on each side, or until they are soft and just browned.

Step 6: Burger buns can be lightly toasted on the grill or in a toaster while the mushrooms are frying.

Step 7: During the final minute of cooking, if preferred, lay a slice of cheese on each Portobello mushroom, allowing it to slightly melt.

Step 8: Apply mayonnaise to the bottom half of each burger bun before assembling the burgers. Add a lettuce leaf, a cheese-topped Portobello mushroom that has been grilled, a tomato slice, and slices of red onion on top.

Step 9: Put the top half of the burger bread on top and, if required, fasten the burger with a toothpick.

Step 10: Enjoy the mouthwatering combination of meaty mushrooms and tasty toppings by serving the Portobello mushroom burgers right away.

Even non-vegetarians will enjoy the flavorful vegetarian choice of these Portobello mushroom burgers. The toppings provide freshness and crunch, while the grilled mushrooms give them a meaty texture and a rich umami flavor. You are welcome to add extra toppings or condiments to the burgers to suit your tastes. Enjoy this hearty and mouthwatering burger substitute!

CHAPTER 5

Filling Snacks

When taking diabetes medication, you used to have to be very careful about snacking. Knowing the best healthy snacks for diabetics might help you avoid going for extended periods of time without eating. In these situations, you run the risk of promoting hypoglycemia, often known as low glucose. Many type 2 diabetic medicines available today avoid addressing that problem. In any case, before making any big changes to your meal routine, it is still wise to first consult with your PCP regarding side effects like low glucose.

If you have diabetes, solid snacking is still important for a variety of reasons. For example, to regulate your hunger so you won't overindulge. When you're hungry, it's easy to succumb to the temptation of packaged snacks that are expertly handled and typically heavy in starches.

However, assuming you typically have go-to sound bites at hand, you'll aim to avoid becoming overly eager, excessively hungry, or overtired. By giving your body the correct combination of vitamins, you can improve both your glucose management and overall wellbeing.

Roasted Chickpeas

Ingredients

- 1 can (15 ounces) of rinsed and drained chickpeas
- Olive oil, 1 tbsp.
- 1 teaspoon of cumin, ground
- A half-teaspoon of smoked paprika
- One-half teaspoon of garlic powder
- ½ teaspoons of salt
- Black pepper, ¼ teaspoon

Directions

Step 1: A baking sheet should be lined with parchment paper and the oven should be preheated to 400°F (200°C).

Step 2: The chickpeas should be rinsed, drained, and then dried with a paper towel to eliminate any extra moisture.

Step 3: Chickpeas should be equally coated in a bowl with olive oil, cumin, smoked paprika, garlic powder, salt, and black pepper.

Step 4: On the prepared baking sheet, distribute the seasoned chickpeas in a single layer.

Step 5: In the preheated oven, roast the chickpeas for 25 to 30 minutes, or until they are crispy and golden brown, shaking the pan halfway through to ensure equal cooking.

Step 6: Before serving, take the oven-roasted chickpeas out of the oven and let them cool slightly.

Step 7: Enjoy the crunchy, protein-rich roasted chickpeas as a snack. For a few days, they can be kept in an airtight container.

An excellent and nutritious snack is roasted chickpeas. They have a pleasant crunch and are crispy on the outside. These protein-rich beans get a delicious boost from the combination of spices. You may eat them as a single snack or add them to salads for more crunch. Enjoy your snacks!

Parfait with Greek Yoghurt and Berries

Ingredient

- Greek yogurt, one cup
- 1 cup of mixed berries, including raspberries, blueberries, and strawberries

- 2 teaspoons of maple syrup or honey
- ¼ cup of cereal

Directions

Step 1: Place ¼ cup of Greek yogurt at the bottom of a dish or glass.

Step 2: To the yogurt, add a layer of mixed berries.

Step 3: Over the berries, drizzle ½ tablespoon of honey or maple syrup.

Step 4: Add another ¼ cup of Greek yogurt, more mixed berries, and one more drizzle of honey or maple syrup before repeating the layers.

Greek yogurt is added as the last layer on top of the parfait.

Granola can be put on top for extra crunch. The healthy and energizing Greek yogurt and berry parfait should be served right away.

A delicious and healthful snack, the Greek yogurt and berry parfait mix the smoothness of Greek yogurt with the sweetness and freshness of a variety of berries. Yogurt, berries, honey or maple syrup, and granola are layered to provide a mouthwatering texture and explosion of flavor.

Any time of the day is a great time to enjoy this snack. Good appetite!

Hummus and Veggie Sticks

Ingredient

- Carrot sticks
- Bell pepper slices in a variety of hues

- Plum tomatoes
- Peas
- Young carrots
- (Homemade or store-bought) hummus

Directions

Step 1: Wash and prepare the vegetables by chopping them into bite-sized pieces or stick-like shapes. To make the snack visually appealing, use a variety of vibrant vegetables.

Step 2: On a big plate or serving tray, arrange the cherry tomatoes and vegetable sticks.

Step 3: In the middle of the platter or close to the vegetable sticks, place a dish of hummus.

Step 4: Serving the veggie sticks with hummus makes for a tasty and healthful snack.

Step 5: Enjoy the delectable combination of crunchy vegetables and creamy hummus by dipping the veggie sticks into the hummus.

Veggie sticks and hummus combine to provide a filling and nutrient-rich snack that is high in fiber, vitamins, and minerals. It's a delicious alternative for both adults and children because the vegetables' crunchy texture pairs well with the hummus's creamy and savory flavor.

In addition to being delicious, this snack is a great way to increase the amount of vegetables in your diet. Enjoy!

Kale Chips Baked

Ingredients

- A bunch of kale, among other things.
- ½ teaspoons of salt, ½ teaspoons garlic powder, and 1 tablespoon olive oil

- (Optional) ¼ teaspoon of paprika

Directions

Step 1: A baking sheet should be lined with parchment paper and the oven should be preheated to 350°F (175°C).

Step 2: The kale leaves should be well-cleaned and dried. Cut the kale leaves into bite-sized pieces and remove the stiff stems.

Step 3: Kale leaves should be mixed with olive oil, salt, garlic powder, and paprika (if used) in a big bowl. Make sure the seasonings are equally distributed throughout the leaves.

Step 4: On the prepared baking sheet, arrange the seasoned kale leaves in a single layer.

Step 5: For about 10-15 minutes, or until the edges are crispy and gently browned, bake the kale chips in the preheated oven. They can burn quickly, so keep an eye on them.

Step 6: Before serving, let the kale chips cool for a few minutes after removing the baking sheet from the oven.

Step 7: Take pleasure in the baked kale chips as a nutritious and crunchy treat.

Kale chips that have been baked are a healthy substitute for regular potato chips. They are high in vitamins and minerals and low in calories.

They have a great flavor from the olive oil and herbs, and the baking process makes them crunchy. To make your special versions, feel free to experiment with other seasonings like chili powder, Parmesan cheese, or lemon zest. Enjoy these delicious and guilt-free kale chips!

Almond Butter Energy Bites

Ingredients

- Rolled oats, 1 cup
- 50 ml of almond butter
- ¼ cup maple syrup or honey
- Ground flaxseed, ¼ cup
- Chopped almonds, ¼ cup
- 14 cups raisins or cranberries that are dried
- Vanilla extract, 1 teaspoon
- A dash of salt

Optional ingredients for rolling: Shredded coconut, cocoa powder, or micro chocolate chips.

Directions

Step 1: Rolling oats, almond butter, honey, maple syrup, ground flaxseed, sliced almonds, dried cranberries, raisins, vanilla essence, and a dash of salt should all be combined in a mixing basin. All the components should be thoroughly mixed.

Step 2: To slightly firm up, place the mixture in the refrigerator for 15 to 30 minutes.

Step 3: After the mixture has cold, take it out and form it into balls that are about an inch in diameter and tiny enough to bite into.

Optional: For more flavor and texture, roll the energy balls in shredded coconut, cocoa powder, or micro chocolate chips.

Step 4: Refrigerate the energy bites for at least an hour to allow them to solidify, then place them on a plate or baking sheet.

Step 5: The almond butter energy balls can be kept in the fridge for up to a week in an airtight container.

Step 6: For a quick energy boost, almond butter energy balls are fantastic. They contain healthy nutrients including flaxseed, almond butter, and oats.

In addition to being tasty, these energy balls are a rich source of fiber, protein, and healthy fats. Take advantage of them as a healthy treat on the go, a pre-workout snack, or an afternoon pick-me-up!

Hard-Bubbled Eggs

Eggs with hard bubbles make a healthy snack for people with diabetes.

They really shine because of their high protein content. 6.3 grams of protein, or the amount found in one large hard-boiled egg, are beneficial for people with diabetes because they help keep your blood sugar levels from rising too high after meals.

One study included 65 people with type 2 diabetes who had two eggs per day for a considerable amount of time.

They had sharp drops in their fasting glucose levels near the end of the review. Additionally, they had reduced hemoglobin A1C, a measure of long-term glucose management.

Eggs can increase satiety, which may help reduce calorie intake and promote weight loss. People with diabetes who lose about 10% of their body weight may be able to successfully achieve infection eradication.

You can enjoy one or two hard-boiled eggs for a snack on their own or dress them up with a substantial topping like guacamole.

Berry-Flavored Yoghurt

For several reasons, yoghurt with berries is a fantastic diabetic-friendly snack.

To start, the anti-cancer compounds in berries may reduce inflammation and prevent damage to pancreatic cells, which are responsible for producing the hormones that lower blood sugar levels.

Additionally, berries are a fantastic source of fiber. For instance, a 1-cup (150 gram) portion of blueberries has 3.6 grams of fiber, which helps slow digestion and stabilize blood sugar levels after a meal.

Another benefit of yoghurt is that it can lower blood sugar levels. This is in part due to the probiotics it contains, which may enhance your body's ability to utilize sugar-containing dietary sources.

Yoghurt is also a good source of protein, which may aid in managing blood sugar levels at any time. Particularly high in protein is Greek yoghurt.

Together, yoghurt and berries taste amazing because the sweetness of the berries helps to counteract the melancholy of the yoghurt. To make a parfait, you can just mix them all together or layer them on top of one another.

A little bundle of Almonds

Almonds are a great snack because they are so nourishing.

A 1-ounce (28-gram) portion of almonds contains more than nutrients and minerals, including 0.6 milligrams of manganese, or 27% of the daily recommended amount, 76.5 milligrams of magnesium, or 18%, and 0.32 milligrams of riboflavin, or 25% of the daily recommended amount.

Almonds may help diabetics control their blood sugar, according to research. In one study, 58 people who remembered almonds for their diets consistently for a while saw a 3% decrease in their prolonged glucose levels.

In another study, 20 adults with diabetes who had 60 grams of almonds every day for a very long time saw a 4% decrease in their levels of insulin, a chemical that, on the off chance that levels are consistently high, may worsen diabetes.

Almonds' ability to help with glucose settling is made possible by the combination of fiber, protein, and solid fats that they contain, all of which play a vital role in diabetes across the board.

Almonds may also improve overall weight management and heart health, both of which are crucial in preventing and treating type 2 diabetes. This is because they lower cholesterol levels.

Almonds are quite calorie-dense, thus it is best to limit your portion to around a little bunch while taking a bite.

Hummus and Vegetables

Smooth chickpeas are used to make hummus. When paired with unrefined vegetables, it tastes wonderful. The two veggies are excellent sources of fiber, nutrients, and minerals, as does hummus.

Additionally, hummus provides a small quantity of protein and fat from a dependable source. These characteristics might help diabetics with glucose regulation.

According to one study, those who ingested at least 1 ounce of hummus at a meal had significantly lower blood sugar and insulin levels than those who only ate white bread.

A few different types of vegetables, such as broccoli, cauliflower, carrots, and ring peppers, can be dipped in hummus to create new dishes.

Avocado

If you have diabetes, eating an avocado might help you control your blood sugar.

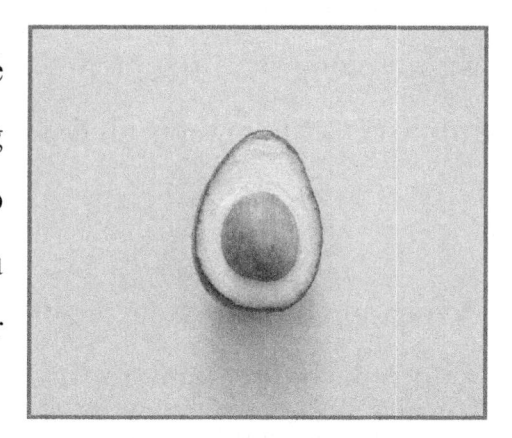

Avocados are a food that diabetes's enjoy because of their high monounsaturated unsaturated fat and fiber content. These factors might prevent a spike in your blood sugar after dinner.

According to one study, persons with type 2 diabetes who continuously remembered sources of monounsaturated unsaturated fats for their weight-control regimens had significant improvements in their glucose levels.

Avocado can be eaten on its own or combined with other ingredients to form guacamole. Since avocados contain a lot of calories, it is best to limit your serving size to one-fourth to one avocado.

Sliced Apples with Peanut Butter

Cut apples combined with nut butter make for a delicious and substantial snack that is ideal for those with diabetes.

Apples are rich in several supplements, including potassium, L-ascorbic acid, and vitamin B minerals from Trusted Sources, while peanut butter contains magnesium and vitamin E from, all of which are proven to help manage diabetes.

The two apples, along with the peanut butter, are also quite high in fiber. One medium apple and two tablespoons (32 grams) of peanut butter together provide about 7 grams of fiber, which is beneficial for controlling hyperglycemia.

Apples have been specifically researched for their potential role in diabetes management by executives. They are known to protect pancreatic cells from damage that frequently destroys diabetes because to the polyphenol cancer prevention compounds they contain.

CHAPTER 6

Enticing Desserts

Avocado with Chocolate Mousse

Ingredients

- 2 ripe avocados are included.
- Cocoa powder, ¼ cup
- ¼ cup honey or maple syrup
- Any other non-dairy milk, or ¼ cup of almond milk
- Vanilla extract, 1 teaspoon

- A dash of salt
- Fresh berries, shredded coconut, and chopped nuts are optional additions.

Directions

Step 1: Avocados should be cut in half, the pits taken out, and the flesh scooped into a food processor or blender.

Step 2: To the blender or food processor, add the cocoa powder, maple syrup or honey, almond milk, vanilla extract, and salt.

Step 3: While processing, scrape down the edges as necessary to ensure a smooth, creamy texture.

Step 4: To suit your tastes, taste the mixture and adjust the sweetness or cocoa amount as necessary.

Step 5: Put the mousse into separate dishes or glasses for serving.

Step 6: Set and chill in the refrigerator for at least an hour. For more texture and flavor, garnish the mousse with fresh berries, shredded coconut, or chopped nuts before serving.

Take pleasure in the decadent and rich chocolate avocado mousse as a healthy dessert alternative.

A delectable delicacy that combines the richness of chocolate with the creamy consistency of avocados is chocolate avocado mousse. It is a pleasure that is devoid of guilt and rich in antioxidants and good fats. In addition to being delicious, this dessert is also vegan, gluten-free, and dairy-free. Enjoy this tasty dessert that will fill you up while also providing your body with nutrients.

Dark Flourless Chocolate Cake

Ingredients

- Eight ounces of chopped dark chocolate are used in the flourless chocolate cake.
- Cubed half a cup of unsalted butter
- Granulated sugar, ¾ cup
- Four big eggs
- Vanilla extract, 1 teaspoon
- A dash of salt
- Powdered sugar, fresh berries, and whipped cream are optional garnishes.

Directions

Step 1: Set the oven's temperature to 350°F (175°C). A 9-inch round cake pan should be greased and lined with parchment paper on the bottom.

Step 2: Butter and the chopped dark chocolate should be combined in a heatproof basin. Make sure the bowl's bottom doesn't touch the water as you place it over a saucepan of simmering water. As soon as the chocolate and butter are melted and smooth, stir occasionally. Take it off the fire and give it a minute to cool.

Step 3: The granulated sugar, eggs, vanilla extract, and salt must all be thoroughly incorporated in a different mixing dish.

Step 4: When the chocolate mixture has completely melted, add it to the egg mixture and whisk it together.

Step 5: Fill the prepared cake pan with the batter, then use a spatula to smooth the top.

Step 6: Bake for 25 to 30 minutes in the preheated oven, or until the rims are golden and the center is just jiggled.

Step 7: The cake should be taken out of the oven and allowed to cool for about 10 minutes in the pan. After that, move it to a wire rack to finish cooling.

Step 8: When the cake has cooled, you can top it with powdered sugar, decorate with fresh berries, or serve it with whipped cream.

Step 9: This flourless chocolate cake is a rich and opulent dessert choice. Slice and serve.

For chocolate lovers, flourless chocolate cake is a delicious treat. This cake has a rich, fudgy texture and a strong chocolate flavor. It is gluten-free because there is no flour, and the use of premium dark chocolate adds antioxidants and a posh flavor. Enjoy this decadent dessert on special occasions or whenever you're in the mood for something sweet with chocolate.

Chia-Raspberry Pudding

Ingredients

- Chia seeds, ¼ cup
- 1 cup non-dairy milk, such as unsweetened almond milk

- 2 teaspoons of honey or maple syrup
- One-half teaspoon of vanilla extract
- Fresh raspberries, half a cup
- Additional fresh raspberries, shredded coconut, and chopped nuts are optional additions.

Directions

Step 1: Combine the chia seeds, almond milk, honey or maple syrup, and vanilla essence in a bowl. To blend, thoroughly stir.

Step 2: Stir the mixture once more to avoid the chia seeds clumping after letting it settle for around 5 minutes.

Step 3: Allow the chia seeds to absorb the liquid and take on the consistency of custard by covering the bowl and placing it in the refrigerator for at least two hours or overnight.

Step 4: Give the chia pudding a thorough toss when it has set to remove any clumps and spread the seeds evenly.

Step 5: Use a fork to mash the fresh raspberries into a chunky puree in a different bowl.

Step 6: Pour chia pudding into serving glasses or bowls first, then pile on crushed raspberries to construct. The layers should be repeated until the glasses or bowls are full.

Step 7: You can add more fresh raspberries, shredded coconut, or chopped nuts on top of the raspberry chia pudding if you like.

Step 8: Enjoy the creamy consistency and delicious flavor of the chilled raspberry chia pudding.

A tasty and healthy treat that is rich in fiber, omega-3 fatty acids, and antioxidants is raspberry chia pudding.

When chia seeds are soaked in almond milk, they become creamy and pudding-like, while the mashed raspberries give a tart and sweet flavor. This dessert is not only filling, but it's also a wonderful way to add nutritious foods to your diet. Enjoy this tasty and revitalizing treat!

Macarons with Coconut

Ingredients

- 3 cups of shredded coconut (unsweetened)
- 6/3 cups of enhanced dense milk
- Two teaspoons of vanilla extract

- 2 enormous egg whites
- ¼ teaspoons of salt
- **Discretionary:** 4 ounces of melted dark chocolate for showering

Directions

Step 1: The stove to 325°F (160°C) before using it. Use material paper to line a baking sheet.

Step 2: Combine the crushed coconut, better-consolidated milk, and vanilla extract in a sizable mixing basin. Mix thoroughly until well-consolidated.

Step 3: Use an electric mixer to thoroughly combine the salt and egg whites in a separate bowl so that hard pinnacles form.

Step 4: Gently fold the egg whites until they are well incorporated into the coconut mixture. Be careful not to allow the egg whites to collapse.

Step 5: Apply appropriate hills of the coconut mixture to the prepared baking sheet using a tablespoon or a treat scoop, spacing them about 2 inches apart.

Step 6: Cook on the preheated burner for 20 to 25 minutes, or until the edges are a brilliant brown color and the macaroons feel somewhat hard to the touch.

Step 7: Allow the macaroons to completely cool on the baking sheet and remove the baking sheet from the grill.

Step 8: When desired, liquefy the dark chocolate in a bowl that can be placed in the microwave for brief intervals until it is smooth. Over the macaroons that have cooled, scatter the melted chocolate.

Step 9: Before serving or storing the coconut macaroons in an impermeable container, let the chocolate set.

Coconut macaroons are a delicious delicacy and a work of art. These delicious snacks have a crisp outside and a mushy, clammy interior. The flavor is rich and generous because of the combination of destroyed coconut and upgraded dense milk. The optional chocolate garnish gives it a debauched feel. Enjoy these delicious coconut macaroons with a magnificent taste or as the perfect end to any feast.

Apple Cinnamon Crumble

Ingredients

- To make the apple cinnamon crumble, prepare 4 cups of peeled, cored, and chopped apples (about 4 medium-sized apples).
- One teaspoon of lemon juice
- ¼ cup of sugar, granulated
- 1 teaspoon of cinnamon powder
- ½ teaspoons of vanilla extract
- ½ cups of ordinary flour
- A half-cup of moved oats
- One-fourth cup of pressed earthy-colored sugar
- ¼ teaspoons of salt
- Cooled, cut into small pieces ¼ cup unsalted spread

Directions

Step 1: The grill should be preheated to 375°F (190°C). Use cooking spray or margarine to grease a baking or pie dish.

Step 2: To prevent sautéing, place the chopped apples and lemon juice in a large basin.

Step 3: The apples should be combined with granulated sugar, ground cinnamon, and vanilla extract. Mix thoroughly to evenly distribute the mixture over the apples.

Step 4: Spread the apple mixture evenly as you transfer it to the prepared baking dish.

Step 5: Add moved oats, ordinary baking flour, brown sugar, and salt to a new bowl. Mix well.

Step 6: To the flour mixture, stir in the hot, diced spread. Blend the margarine into the dry ingredients with your fingers or a cake shaper until the mixture resembles coarse bits.

Step 7: Spread the crumbled mixture evenly over the apples in the baking dish.

Step 8: For about 30-35 minutes, or until the garnish is brilliantly brown and the apples are tender, heat in the prepared grill.

Step 9: Remove the apple cinnamon crumble from the grill and allow it to cool briefly before serving.

Warm apple cinnamon crumble can be served simply, with whipped cream, a dollop of vanilla frozen yogurt, or all three.

A comforting and delicious dish that showcases warm cinnamon and juicy apples is apple cinnamon crumble. Each nibble gets a nice smash from the rich crumbling topping.

This pastry is perfect for cozy gatherings or as a sweet treat throughout the autumn season. Take a bite of this delectable apple cinnamon crumble and enjoy the fantastic combination of apples and cinnamon!

Cookies with Lemon Poppy Seeds

Ingredients

- 2 cups of ordinary flour
- Granulated sugar, 2/3 cup
- Poppy seeds, 2 tablespoons
- Baking powder, two teaspoons
- ½ tsp. baking soda
- ¼ teaspoons of salt

- Buttermilk, one cup
- ½ cup of liquefied and cooled unsalted spread
- 2 large eggs
- Two lemons
- Lemon juice, one
- One teaspoon of vanilla extract

Directions

Step 1: The stove should be preheated to 375°F (190°C). Paper liners or cooking spray can be used to grease the biscuit cups in a biscuit pan.

Step 2: Mix the flour, sugar, poppy seeds, baking powder, baking soda, and salt in a large bowl.

Step 3: Buttermilk, liquefied spread, eggs, lemon zing, lemon juice, and vanilla concentrate should all be combined in a separate bowl.

Step 4: Fill the dry fixings with the wet fixings, then gently press the two together until they have just been consolidated. Be careful not to over-blend; a few knots are acceptable.

Step 5: Divide the player evenly among the previously placed biscuit cups, filling each one to about 3/4 capacity.

Step 6: Around 18 to 20 minutes of heating time on the preheated stove, or until a toothpick inserted into the center of a biscuit comes out clean.

Step 7: Remove the biscuits from the grill and allow them to cool for a few seconds in the tin before transferring them to a wire rack to completely cool.

The lemon poppy seed biscuits are a wonderful breakfast option or a tasty snack.

These delicate, tender biscuits with poppy seeds are bursting with sour lemon flavor. Each bite is brilliantly smashed by the poppy seeds.

These biscuits are perfect for a quick breakfast or enjoyed with tea in the late afternoon. They have a vibrant and zesty flavor thanks to the stimulating lemon zing and juice. Enjoy these delicious biscuits whenever you want as a wonderful treat!

CHAPTER 7

Drinks and Beverages

A Zingy Lemonade

Ingredients

- 4 to 6 lemons
- 1 cup sugar, granulated
- Six mugs of cold water
- 3D squares of ice
- Lemon slices for adornment (at your discretion)
- (Optional) Mint leaves for decoration

Directions

Step 1: To make fresh lemon juice, juice the lemons. Lemon juice, about 1 cup, is needed.

Step 2: Break down the granulated sugar in 1 cup of hot water in a pitcher. Mix thoroughly to completely dissolve the sugar.

Step 3: Mix thoroughly after adding the lemon juice to the pitcher.

Step 4: Five more cups of cold water should be added and combined.

Step 5: Taste the lemonade and, as desired, adjust the sweetness or pungency by adding additional lemon juice or sugar.

Step 6: Before serving, add ice cubes in solid shapes to the pitcher or each glass.

Alternately, add a lemon slice and a sprig of fresh mint to each glass.

Step 7: Enjoy the tangy and revitalizing flavors of the cooling lemonade when served.

When you need a revitalizing beverage, such as on warm late-spring days, lemonade is a piece of art and a revitalizing refreshment. You can adjust the pleasantness and poignancy of this handcrafted lemonade recipe as you see fit. With each sip of this delicious and energizing lemonade, you'll feel more energized.

Note: For a twist on the traditional recipe, you can also experiment with different lemonade kinds by adding flavors like strawberry, raspberry, or mint.

Green Detox Smoothie

Ingredients

- Spinach, 1 cup
- ½ of a cucumber, sliced and stripped
- A sliced and cored half of a green apple
- A half-ripe banana
- Squeezed half of a lemon
- Chia seeds, one tablespoon
- 1 cup almond or other non-dairy milk, unsweetened

Optional: Ice blocks, honey, or maple syrup for sweetness

Directions

Step 1: Put all of the ingredients in a blender.

Step 2: Rapidly blend until rich and silky.

Step 3: When desired, add honey or maple syrup to the smoothie for more sweetness.

Step 4: Add a small group of ice solid forms as needed, then stir again until thoroughly combined.

Step 5: Pour the green smoothie for detoxification into a glass and serve immediately.

The healthy ingredients in the green detox smoothie include spinach, cucumber, apple, and chia seeds. It's a fantastic way to increase the number of greens you eat and increase your daily intake of fiber, nutrients, and minerals. Bananas provide consistent pleasantness and a rich surface, while the addition of lemon juice adds an energizing punch. Enjoy this energizing and substantial smoothie as a revitalizing beverage, a sustaining snack, or a replacement before or after exercise.

CHAPTER 8

Hydration beyond Water

In general, hydration is important for our bodies to function best. Maintaining a healthy liquid intake is essential for our bodies to function normally.

Our hydration affects our blood, which carries nutrients and oxygen to the cells, as well as our kidneys, which remove waste. A very well-hydrated body also ensures joint flexibility, eye oil, processing efficiency, and strong, radiant skin.

Additionally, liquids help direct internal heat levels, which is important in a warm atmosphere like ours. Even a minor decrease in hydration levels can have major consequences, so it's important to replenish any water lost through perspiration, urination, and exercise.

Without water, the human body can survive for three to four days. When side effects like migraine, drowsiness, unpleasant fixation, parched mouth, and profoundly darkened poop appear, you realize you wish to tank up.

Although water is the finest hydration, there are several more ways to get enough fluids in your system.

How to Maintain Body Hydration

1. Adding New Natural Items.

Water produced naturally including the entire integrity of the natural product, adding new natural items to your water bottles, such as orange slices, strawberry bits, or lemon rings, increases the nutrition content. L-ascorbic acid, substances that fight cancer, flavonoids, and minerals like potassium help you stay more hydrated.

2. **Add some zest.**

Adding some zest to your water will give it all of its medicinal benefits. Ajwain (Carom Seed) aids in general digestion, Jeera (Cumin Plant) helps with tooting, Dhania (Coriander Plant) seeds help with hypothyroid side effects, and Saunf (Fennel

Plant) promotes absorption and prevents corrosiveness.

3. Soups.

An efficient way to increase the entry of vegetable fibers and maintain hydration is to make cold or warm soup with fresh vegetables. It aids in regulating excessive calorie intake between meals while providing essential minerals, nutrients, and cell reinforcements. Cold tomato and cucumber soups have a delicious flavor.

4. Vegetable Juices.

Vegetable juices, especially those that are blended, help to hydrate while maintaining the integrity of the vegetable. In this approach, spinach juice increases the amount of potent cell reinforcements like beta-carotene and L-ascorbic acid. Beets add potassium, folate, and manganese, while carrots add biotin, potassium, and vitamin A.

5. Dairy Choices.

Dairy Choices like Lassi, Chaas, and skim milk all contribute to well-being. Although they do add calories, the vitamins they give your regular dinners are essential. Protein, calcium, polyphenols, phosphorus, and, if you choose enhanced versions, vitamin D. Probiotics, which are essential for digestive health, are also added when dairy products are matured to make yogurt or Dahi.

6. Coffee and Tea.

Coffee and tea when used sparingly, these beverages are excellent. Both include cancer preventatives. Green tea has been shown to significantly improve our daily eating habits and health. Separately, green tea and dark tea are both abundant sources of catechins and theaflavins. Espresso is a plentiful source of flavonoids, which exhibit strong cell-reinforcing activity.

7. New traditional beverages.

There are several fantastic ways to stay hydrated, including kanji, Bael sherbet, aam panna, sattu, and rice/ragi kanji. They have been demonstrated to benefit gut health, which results in improved resistance. Rich in cell reinforcements, these drinks also exhibit a cooling effect on our bodies.

The key caveat is that one should limit additional sugars.

8. **Summer soil items are dripping with liquid.**

Our dinners are made more hydrating by the water content of hiya, tori, and tienda. 90% of the water is in natural goods like watermelons and melons. These whole soil products hydrate the body even though they are not "fluids".

Soft drinks, commercial fruit juice, and caffeinated beverages are all excellent hydration, but the drawback is that they are also very high in sugar. Soft drinks are not a good option for hydration because they are high in calories and lack supplements. Financially motivated organic product squeezes also contain additional sugar and don't improve nutrition. Juice from a new organic product is a wise choice.

Think beyond water to properly hydrate yourself this late spring and throughout the year. As a general guideline, our body needs 35 to 45 ml/kg of liquid each day; make sure you drink sensibly and choose healthy foods.

CHAPTER 9

BONUS FEATURES

Food Shopping Guide:

Filling Your Cooler and Storeroom for Success

Filling your refrigerator and pantry with wholesome ingredients is the way to go if you want to maintain a healthy and glucose-friendly way of living.

You'll be able to produce delicious and well-balanced feasts if your kitchen is well stocked, saving you from having to make frequent trips to the grocery store. Here is a guide to help you load your refrigerator and storage space to make progress:

Basics of a Storage Room:

- Whole grains include whole wheat pasta, whole grain bread, quinoa, oats, and rice with an earthy hue.
- Beans, lentils, and chickpeas, either dried or in a can.
- Almonds, pecans, chia seeds, flaxseeds, and sunflower seeds are among the nuts and seeds.

- Extra virgin olive oil, avocado oil, and coconut oil are all good oils.
- Basil, oregano, turmeric, cinnamon, cumin, and paprika are among the spices and flavors.
- Vegetable, chicken, or animal stocks for flavorful soups and stews are low-sodium options.
- Flexible for sauces and stews are canned tomatoes and tomato glue.
- Almond margarine or peanut butter, preferably natural varieties without sugars.
- Kinds of vinegar: rice vinegar, balsamic vinegar, and apple juice vinegar for marinades and sauces.
- Low-sodium soy sauce or tamari: Gives marinades and sautés flavor.

Basics of a Refrigerator:

- New vegetables include carrots, broccoli, tomatoes, bell peppers, mixed greens (spinach, kale), and spinach.
- Berries, apples, oranges, bananas, and grapes for smoothies and snacking are recent natural products.
- Lean proteins include fish (salmon, cod), eggs, tofu, chicken, turkey, and poultry.
- Choose unsweetened variations like almond milk or oat milk if you're drinking dairy or plant-based milk.
- **Greek yogurt or vegan options:** Options high in protein for breakfast or snacks.
- **Sauces:** Low-sugar mustard, salsa, low-fat or light salad dressings, and low-sugar ketchup.

- Parsley, cilantro, and basil are three new spices that can be used to flavor food.
- Choose options like feta, mozzarella, or curds instead of reduced-fat cheddar.
- **Drinks with less or no sugar:** Water, herbal teas, and sparkling water for hydration.
- Parsley, cilantro, and basil are three new spices that can be used to flavor food.

Make sure to regularly check expiration dates and, when necessary, refresh your refrigerator and storage space. You'll be prepared to prepare a variety of delicious and nutritious dinners that support your glucose-accommodating way of life if you keep these staples close at hand. Shopping and cooking bliss!

Cooking Techniques and Kitchen Tips

1. **Keep your blades sharp:**

Cutting and hacksawing fasteners are easier and safer with a sharp blade. Spend money on a blade sharpener or often have your blades professionally polished.

2. **Prepare Ahead:**

Prepare the fixings in advance to save time during the preparation of the meal by chopping vegetables, planning the fixings, and marinating the proteins well in advance. For easy access, place prepared fixings in the ice chest's airtight sections.

3. **Citrus juice can be used to prevent cooking:**

Squeeze lemon or lime juice over fruits or vegetables that will typically oxidize, such as apples or avocados, to slow down oxidation.

4. **Maintain freshness of spices:**

Place fresh herbs, such as parsley or cilantro, in a glass of water and cover completely with a plastic bag. To extend their freshness, store them in the refrigerator.

5. Excess fixings can be frozen:

If you have excess spices, stock, or sauces, put them in an ice block dish and freeze them. When necessary, jump out of the 3D tiles to add flavor to continuing recipes.

6. Use suitable cooking oil:

Since different oils have varying smoke points, choose the right oil for your cooking method. For high-heat cooking, use oils with high smoke points, such as canola or avocado oil, and reserve delicate oils, such as extra virgin olive oil, for dressings or low-heat cooking.

7. Taste as you go:

You are welcome to taste your food as it is cooking and adjust the preparation as necessary. You will be helped in achieving the optimal flavor balance by doing this.

8. Replace with superior alternatives:

Replace high-carb or sugary ingredients with more wholesome alternatives. Use Greek yogurt instead of harsh cream, for instance, or substitute zucchini noodles or cauliflower rice for traditional grains.

9. **Use a meat thermometer:**

Use a meat thermometer to ensure that the meat is cooked to the proper temperature. This prevents overcooking or undercooking, ensuring sanitization and perfect flavor.

10. **Maintain Cleanliness:**

Keep your kitchen organized and spotless by washing dishes, wiping down surfaces, and taking care of supplies as you cook. As a result, there is less mess and cleanup is much simpler.

11. **Look at many options for spices and flavors:**

To improve the quality of your food, make sure to experiment with new spices and flavors. They may give even the simplest dishes depth and complexity.

Use the mise en place technique to ensure that "all things are where they should be." Before you start cooking, gather and organize all of the ingredients and equipment you'll need. As a result, the cooking process is more efficient and enjoyable.

Remember that cooking is an art that takes creativity and individuality into account. While preparing delectable and wholesome meals in your kitchen, feel free to contemplate, rely on your taste buds, and indulge!

Dinner Planning Procedures and Layouts

The planning of meals is a crucial component of maintaining a balanced and glucose-friendly diet. It helps you stay organized, make time-saving decisions, and make wiser eating choices. To get you started, consider these formats and strategies for planning dinner:

1. **Weekly Meal Planning Format:**

Create a weekly meal planner with categories for breakfast, lunch, dinner, and snacks.

Every day, fill your mind with feast ideas that balance proteins, vegetables, whole grains, and healthy fats. To prepare for the coming week, think about bulk cooking and extras.

2. Organizing a subject-based feast:

Give each day of the week a different topic, such as Meatless Monday, Taco Tuesday, Sautéed Food Wednesday, etc.

Create your meals around the subject, incorporating a variety of ingredients and flavors while keeping them glucose-friendly.

3. Fixings Turn:

To save money and prevent food waste, schedule dinners around sporadic and inexpensive fixings.

Shift your focus to meats, veggies, and grains to ensure variety and boost the nutritional benefits.

4. Cooler Dinner Preparation:

Set out a day to prepare and freeze meals in advance. To keep track of the things and expiration dates, use cooler well-disposed holders and names.

5. **Pre-Made Feast Packs:**

Gather feast units in advance with estimated ingredients for quick and easy cooking on busy days.

For enhanced comfort, keep these packs in the cooler or ice chest.

6. **Mobile phone Websites and Applications:**

Use meal planning software or websites that provide personalized menu plans and dish recommendations based on your nutritional preferences and glycemic targets.

Combining your meal plan with a shopping list can ensure that you have all of the necessary ingredients on hand.

For efficient food shopping, organize your list by categories (produce, dairy, storage, etc.).

7. **Careful Piece Control:**

Pay attention to piece sizes to keep an eye on glucose levels. Reduce portions and prevent overindulgence by using smaller dishes and bowls.

Plan dinners that can be easily transformed into different dishes using extras. Consider adding grilled vegetables to a frittata or other dish.

8. Treat preparation:

Allow yourself occasional snacks during your feast so that you don't feel deprived.

Remember that the planning of a feast can be flexible and tailored to your preferences and way of life. The goal is to improve overall prosperity and glucose management by making your eating habits more intentional and realistic. Wonderful planning of the feast!

Tips for Cooking with Glucose in Mind

There are certain tips and tricks you may use about cooking that is glucose-accommodating to improve and adapt your feasts. Here are some tips to keep in mind:

1. Choose Whole, Natural Food kinds:

Whenever possible, choose whole, natural food kinds. These include organic foods, fresh produce, whole grains, lean proteins, and healthy fats.

Whole food options are typically lower in added sugars and greater in vitamins, making them a better choice for controlling blood sugar levels.

2. Focus on fiber:

Choose whole grains, veggies, and other high-fiber food types for your feasts. Fiber slows down the absorption of glucose, helping to prevent glucose spikes. Additionally, it enhances a sense of wholeness and improves stomach-related health.

3. **Limit Refined Carbohydrates:**

Limit or avoid foods high in refined starches, such as white bread, white rice, and sweet treats. These foods have the potential to quickly increase blood glucose levels. Choose whole grain products like quinoa, earthy-colored rice, and whole wheat bread once all is said and done.

Lean protein sources, such as chicken, turkey, fish, tofu, and vegetables, should be incorporated into your meals. Protein controls glucose levels and improves satiety, which can help prevent overeating and control glucose levels.

4. **Effective Cooking Techniques:**

Use effective cooking methods like grilling, baking, steaming, or sautéing with little to no oil. Avoid deep sautéing or broiling, which can increase the number of unnecessary calories and unhealthy fats in your meals.

5. **Control Part Sizes:**

Pay attention to segment sizes to avoid consuming excessive amounts of calories and sugar. To help with segment control, use measuring cups or a food scale. Remember that even high-quality food sources might contribute to elevated glucose levels if consumed in large quantities.

6. Investigate many options concerning spices and flavors:

To improve the flavor of your dishes without using sugar or unsavory sauces, use spices, flavors, and other flavorings. Investigate alternative perspectives on various spices and flavors to give your feasts depth and complexity.

7. Keep Hydrated:

Throughout the day, consume a lot of water. Remaining hydrated can enhance overall well-being and may aid in maintaining stable blood sugar levels.

8. **Traditional Mealtimes:**

Schedule regular dinnertimes and make an effort to stick to a consistent eating schedule. This can help regulate glucose levels and prevent extreme variations.

Monitor your starch intake and see a registered dietician or medical services expert to determine the right amount of carbohydrates for your unique needs.

Remember that to create a personalized meal plan that meets your unique dietary requirements and glycemic control goals, you must speak with a medical services expert or registered dietitian.

Selection of Low-Glycemic Fixtures

Choosing low-glycemic ingredients is a crucial step in managing blood sugar levels. Here are some suggestions for selecting low-glycemic fixings:

1. Choose whole grain options:

Whole Grain options such as quinoa, earthy colored rice, whole wheat bread, and whole grain pasta. Compared to refined grains, these have a lower glycemic index.

2. Non-Boring veggies:

When planning your dinners, keep in mind to include a variety of non-boring veggies, such as mixed greens, broccoli, cauliflower, zucchini, bell peppers, and cucumbers. These vegetables have few carbohydrates and barely alter blood sugar levels.

3. Veggies:

Include veggies in your feast like lentils, chickpeas, and black beans. They provide a lot of fiber and protein, which can help control blood sugar levels.

4. Lean Proteins:

Choose low-fat dairy products, skinless chicken, turkey, fish, and other lean protein sources. Protein can help with satiety and barely influence glucose levels.

Include sources of healthy fats such as avocados, nuts, seeds, and olive oil. These fats slow down absorption and help keep blood sugar levels in check.

5. Organic foods with a low sugar content:

Choose foods like berries, apples, pears, and citrus that are naturally low in sugar. Compared to tropical organic foods like bananas and pineapples, these organic items have a lower glycemic index.

Use normal sugars like erythritol, stevia, or the purest natural product in place of regular sugar. The glucose levels are barely impacted by these carbohydrates.

6. **Spices and flavors:**

Use flavors and spices like cinnamon, turmeric, ginger, and garlic to improve the quality of your meals. A few flavors that are reminiscent of cinnamon have been shown to help control glucose levels.

7. **Dairy Options:**

If you decide to go this route, choose unsweetened options like soy milk, almond milk, or coconut milk. Be mindful of added sugars in upgraded versions.

Water should always be your first choice for hydration. Avoid sugary drinks including soda, fruit juice squeezes, and enhanced beverages because they can raise your blood sugar levels.

When incorporating these low-glycemic fixings into your dinners, keep in mind that it's important to take section sizes and individual dietary requirements into account. Working with a licensed dietician or medical professional can provide personalized guidance for effectively managing your blood sugar levels.

Alternatives that Work for Sugar and High-Carb Fixings

You can substitute other good ingredients for less sugar and high-carb ingredients when creating dishes that are glucose-friendly. These are a few ideas:

1. **Regular Sugars:** Replace refined sugar with regular sugars that have an impact on blood glucose levels. Here are a few options:

- **Stevia:** A calorie-free sugar derived from the stevia plant.

- **Priest Organic item:** A sugar substitute with no calories that can replace sugar. Sugar alcohol with little effect on calories and glucose is erythritol.

- **Organic Substance Purees:** To give dishes regular pleasantness, use organic ingredients that have been mashed or pureed, such as dates, fruit purée, or bananas. They can be added to already-made goods or used as garnish on yogurt, cereal, and hotcakes.

- **Unsweetened Fruit Purée:** In baking recipes, use unsweetened fruit purée instead of oil or margarine. While reducing the overall fat content, it increases wetness and pleasantness in general.

- **Almond or coconut flour:** It can be used as a substitute for refined wheat flour in recipes. These flours are suitable for cooking with glucose since they have a lower sugar content and a higher fiber content.

- **Greek Yogurt:** In place of bitter cream or heavy cream, use plain, unsweetened Greek yogurt in recipes. While adding protein and providing a smooth surface, it is lower in fat and carbohydrates.

- **Cauliflower Rice:** For a lower-carb alternative, use cauliflower rice in place of regular rice. It is very likely to be used as a base for mixed greens servings without grains, in pan-sears, rice-based recipes, or in dishes that use rice.

- **Zucchini Noodles:** Replace regular pasta with zucchini noodles, sometimes known as 'zoodles'. They are a low-carb alternative that can be used in many pasta meals.

- **Nut Margarine:** Use regular nut spreads like almond or peanut butter rather than dips or spreads with a lot of added sugar. They provide protein and good lipids without adding extra sugars.

- **Unsweetened Coconut Milk:** Replace dairy milk or better beverages with unsweetened coconut milk. It frequently appears in curries, smoothies, and other cuisines.

- **Spices and flavors:** Instead of relying on added sugars or flavors high in salt, switch to foods that use spices and flavors. Examine many options for spices like cinnamon, vanilla bean paste, nutmeg, and ginger.

While using better choices, keep in mind that segment control is still essential. Additionally, it's generally a good idea to speak with a registered dietitian or medical services expert to ensure that these replacements are in line with your unique dietary needs and wellness goals.

Top 5 Hacks to reduce Blood Sugar Increase

1. Take a Green Appetizer:

Fiber comes first, then the greens. Any vegetable will do, including coleslaw, asparagus, courgette, peppers, broccoli, lettuce, and tomatoes. Two cups of spinach, five bumped artichoke hearts, vinegar, and olive oil are my favorite ingredients.

One of my followers regularly consumed a platter of barbecued broccoli with hot sauce and salt before supper and lost 88 pounds in a year and a half.

2. Have some vinegar first:

In one study, taking vinegar before meals helped people who were trying to reduce weight do so by losing twice as much weight as those who didn't. Just consume one spoonful of vinegar with a beautiful specimen a few moments before dining.

3. Start with a teaspoon and progress:

I prefer Apple juice vinegar because it is more cordial. Can't bring yourself to drink it?

Concerning your green beginning, add a vinegar-based dressing.

4. Have a tasty morning:

Have you ever noticed that after eating flapjacks and maple syrup, you become energized again by 10 am? Your glucose levels are influenced by the meals you eat first thing in the morning all day long.

Greek yogurt, tofu, pork, fish, cheddar, cream cheddar, protein powder, nuts, nut spread, seeds, and eggs are other delicious and appetizing morning additions to pair with your vegetables.

5. Following a meal, move about:

That Sunday-after-the-broil walk is a great idea. Since practice prevents the accumulation of glucose in the body, 10 to 20 minutes are sufficient to reduce glucose rise. You can perform 10 minutes of any exercise you enjoy, whether it's yoga or strength training.

Cooking Techniques for Glucose Management

The cooking techniques you employ can affect the nutritional content of your dinners when it comes to controlling your blood sugar. The following cooking techniques can help maintain steady blood sugar levels:

1. **Steaming:**

The delicate cooking technique of steaming preserves the natural flavors, additives, and surface of food sources. Vegetables notably benefit from it. Compared to boiled or seared options, steamed veggies have a lower glycemic index.

2. **Barbecuing:**

Barbecuing is a good cooking technique that enhances flavor without calling for excessive amounts of fats or oils. Lean proteins like chicken, fish, and tofu are often used with it. By allowing fat to drip out from the food while grilling, calories, and fat content are reduced.

3. **Cooking or Baking:**

Without using excessive amounts of oil, cooking or baking food items on the stove can enhance their flavors and surfaces. For fish, lean meats, and veggies, it is a sensible approach. Broiling brings out the natural sweetness of vegetables and can enhance the depth of the various slices of meat.

4. **Pan-Searing:**

Pan-searing is the process of quickly frying tiny, scaled-down pieces of food in a little amount of oil at a high heat. It is a fantastic way to keep vegetables' natural crunch and color while cutting down on cooking time. Use little oil and choose healthy oils like coconut or olive oil.

5. Sautéing:

Sautéing is the quick preparation of food in a small amount of oil at medium-high heat. For vegetables, lean meats, and fish, a flexible cooking method can be used. Use only a small amount of healthy oil, and avoid using excessive amounts of high-sodium sauces or flavors.

6. Poaching:

Poaching is the delicate preparation of food in a liquid at a low temperature, such as water or stock. It is typically used for organic food, eggs, chicken, and fish. Without adding extra fat or calories, poaching preserves the food's natural flavors and additives.

7. Cooking:

Cooking is a process of food preparation that exposes food to intense coordination from the highest point of the stove. A quick cooking method can give food a fresh or caramelized surface. Use lean proteins, such as fish or skinless chicken, and keep an eye out for any marinades or sauces to avoid added sugars.

8. Slow cooking:

Slow cooking entails cooking food slowly over an extended period at a low temperature. Planning soups, stews, and braised foods can benefit from using this technique. Slow cooking enables flavors to develop without the use of excessive fats or oils.

Remember that it's crucial to choose healthy ingredients, monitor your meal's segment sizes, and pay attention to the overall balance of your feast while cooking for glucose management.

Control of Segments and Dinner Planning

For maintaining stable glucose levels and managing general health, segment management and meal planning are crucial. Here are some tips for segment control and dinner attendees who want to aid with glucose regulation:

1. **Understand Piece Sizes:**

Learn more about appropriate piece sizes for different nutrition classes. Make sure you're eating the right amounts of sugars, proteins, fats, and veggies by using measuring cups, a food scale, or visual aids.

2. **Make Adjusted Meals:**

Every dinner should have a balance of carbohydrates, proteins, healthy fats, and fiber-rich veggies. This mixture can support energy while helping to control blood sugar levels.

3. **Use a More Subdued Plate:**

Present your meals on more subdued plates and bowls. This visual gimmick can help you feel content in more modest parts.

4. **Partially Fill Your Plate with Colorful Vegetables:**

Salad greens, broccoli, peppers, and zucchini are colorful vegetables that are low in calories and carbohydrates but high in fiber and nutrients. To add heft and increase satiety, place these vegetables on half of your plate.

5. **Measure the starches in your diet**:

This is because carbohydrates have a significant impact on blood sugar levels. To properly divide carb-rich food sources like grains, bland vegetables, and natural goods, use measuring cups or a food scale.

6. Lean Protein Options:

Lean protein options like; skinless chicken, turkey, fish, tofu, veggies, and low-fat dairy, should all be included in your dinners. Protein controls blood sugar levels and promotes fullness.

7. Solid Fat Serving Sizes:

Solid fat serving sizes should be observed because, in addition to being substantial, they are also calorie-dense. Keep in mind that foods like nuts, seeds, avocados, and oils come in part measurements. To keep calorie intake under control, stick to appropriate serving sizes.

8. **Pre-Party Bites:**

Pre-segment your snacks into individual servings if you anticipate indulging in them frequently. This can help you adhere to proper portion sizes and prevent mindless munching.

9. **Dinner Preparation:**

Plan your meals to ensure balanced and controlled portions. Planning your meal should take into account your daily calorie and starch goals. This instruction can also help you make wiser decisions and steer clear of impolite food selections.

10. Keep a Food Journal:

Record your meals, portion sizes, and blood sugar levels in a food journal. This might help you distinguish between different examples and adjust your meal plan as necessary.

11. Look for Skilled Direction:

Collaborate with a medical professional or enlisted dietician who knows about diabetes or glucose management. They can provide tailored guidance on segment control, meal planning, and generally speaking nutrition for your unique needs.

Remember that every person's nutritional needs and portion sizes may vary, so it's important to speak with a medical services expert for personalized recommendations. You can support overall well-being and maintain stable glucose levels by practicing portion management and meal planning.

Equipment and Devices for Glucose-Compatible Cooking

Having the proper tools and equipment can make the process of cooking for people with diabetes easier and more productive. Several tools and equipment listed below can be helpful:

1. **Estimating Cups and Spoons:**

Accurate meal estimating is essential for glucose control, especially when it comes to carbs. To precisely package fixings, use measuring cups and spoons.

A food scale is useful for weighing ingredients, especially when it comes to carbs, proteins, and lipids. More accurate estimates are provided, and segment control is aided.

2. Non-Stick Cookware:

By requiring less oil while cooking, non-stick pans and pots reduce the overall fat content of the food. They also facilitate cooking without having to stay, which is advantageous because it reduces the need for additional fats.

3. Liner Bin:

Steaming vegetables is a reliable method of preparation, and a liner container stores ingredients and surfaces. It takes into account delicate cooking without the need for additional oils or fats.

A stove can be used for searing, simmering, and broiling. It can be used to produce a variety of meals that are suitable for people with diabetes, including lean proteins, cooked vegetables, and prepared low-carb foods.

4. Blender or Food Processor:

A blender or food processor is useful for pureeing agricultural products, blending smoothie ingredients, and creating healthy sauces and dressings. They can help you include more nutrient-dense ingredients in your dinners.

5. Slow Cooker:

A slow cooker is ideal for quickly and easily preparing filling and delicious meals. It takes into account long, slow cooking, which can enhance flavors and soften lean meats without calling for excessive amounts of fats or oils.

6. Spiralizer:

A spiralizer is a useful tool for creating vegetable noodles, sometimes known as "zoodles." It is frequently used to replace high-carb pasta with low-carb alternatives, hence increasing the amount of veggies in your dinners.

7. **Juicer:**

If you enjoy fresh squeeze, a juicer might be beneficial for creating your juice concoctions from novel green foods. When drinking juice, be mindful of the sugar content and component measurements.

8. **Food Capacity Compartments:**

Having a variety of food storage containers can help with portion control and meal preparation. Use them to keep leftovers or feasts that have been prepared in advance.

Remember that while these tools and equipment may be useful, they are not necessary for cooking that accommodates glucose. Even so, you can still prepare delicious and satisfying meals using standard kitchen appliances. Focus on choosing nutritious ingredients, practicing portion control, and employing appropriate cooking techniques to aid with glucose control.

FAQs

How can I have delicious dinners while managing my blood sugar levels?

- Focus on maintaining a healthy diet that includes lean proteins, complex carbohydrates, and good fats.

- Control of segments is crucial. Concentrate on segment estimations while avoiding indulgence.

- Integrate routine tasks into your daily calendar to help you keep an eye on your blood sugar levels.

- For specialized guidance, speak with a hired nutritionist or medical expert.

Which common ingredients can sugar be replaced within recipes?

- Regular sugars can be substituted with erythritol, stevia, or priest natural product separately.

- Smashed bananas or unsweetened fruit purée can give a natural sweetness and moisture to baked goods.

- Without adding sugar, cinnamon or vanilla concentrate can enhance some types of foods.

What can I do to prevent my food from sticking to the dish?

- Make sure your container has been properly warmed before adding any fixings.

- Use sound cooking oil in moderation or non-stick cooking spray.

- Avoid packing the container too tightly so that food steams rather than singes.

If my food tastes too strongly flavored, what more can I do?

- By adding corrosive (lemon juice or vinegar), pleasantness (a little sugar or honey), or weakening the dish with unsalted ingredients, you can counteract the pungency.

- To aid in spreading the flavor, think about adding more grains, proteins, or veggies.

How can I improve the flavor of my dinners without using excessive salt or sugar?

- Investigate many options for using spices, flavors, and aromatics to improve your foods' standard varieties.

- Integrate citrus zest or juice for a burst of innovation.

- For more depth, add low-sodium stocks, vinegar, or locally-made marinades.

My heated goods come out thick or lacking moisture. How can I improve them further?

- Make sure you are accurately calculating your ingredients, especially flour, which can surely be compressed.

- Include moisturizing ingredients in your meals, such as fruit purée, yogurt, or buttermilk.

- To avoid overcooking, adjust the temperature and baking time.

How might I prepare my feast to save time and maintain mental attention while adhering to my glucose-friendly diet?

- Set up a specific day or time each week to prepare dinner.

- Dinners should be prepared in advance, divided into portions, and stored in the refrigerator or freezer.

- To keep parts separate and up to date, use compartmentalized holders.

My vegetables often come out soggy. How can I prevent this?

- Use shorter cooking periods or opt for techniques like steaming or pan-searing to avoid overcooking veggies.

- Vegetables should be briefly blanched in bubbling water before being transferred to an ice shower to maintain freshness.

How can I tell if a recipe is appropriate for my glucose-friendly eating plan?

- Look for recipes that emphasize whole, natural ingredients, lean proteins, high-fiber carbohydrates, and healthy fats.

- Check the nutritional information, such as the total carbohydrates, fiber content, and added sugars.

- Investigate several options for recipe modifications, such as replacing high-carb ingredients with lower-carb alternatives.

- If everything else fails, seek out specialized advice and guidance on controlling your glucose levels through nutrition from a registered dietician or medical services expert.

Remember that everyone may have different nutritional preferences and needs, so it's important to figure out what works best for you. Be cautious, keep yourself informed, and don't be afraid to experiment in the kitchen.

Exactly how healthy are smoothies for you?

Indeed! This mythological snake smoothie recipe uses organic ingredients and is full of healthy ingredients without any additional sugar. It has a lot of protein and fiber to keep you feeling satisfied and full. It's packed bursting with nutrients and minerals, and it's a remarkable way to quickly, easily, and delectably increase your diet of green foods.

Could you ever prepare smoothies pretty early?

Smoothies are best consumed right after you make them because as soon as a natural product starts to oxidize, its nutrients start to release. If you have excess, place them in a sealed container in the cooler and keep them there for up to 24 hours.

How can I reduce the smoothie's calorie count?

Try substituting one of the bananas with an extra legendary Serpent natural product in the smoothie instead of using two bananas for two servings. Coconut water can also be used in place of almond milk, which will cut calories while enhancing the tropical flavor.

This legendary serpent smoothie is healthy, energizing, and very gorgeous. I sincerely hope you give it a try for both you and your children.

A brand-new, delicious, and excellent smoothie for success!

Can I ever Freeze my espresso banana smoothie?

Make a cooler pack out of this espresso smoothie! I adore preparing smoothie packs in the refrigerator for a quick and easy breakfast or snack.

The sliced banana, oats, espresso (solid forms would be good), cocoa, protein powder, and cinnamon should all be placed in a quart-sized cooler bag before freezing.

When ready to make, add the milk of choice and the cooler's contents to a quick blender and blend until smooth. Start slowly and increase the speed so the frozen fixings have a chance to slightly separate.

Is this coffee smoothie substantial enough to serve for breakfast?

With less than 300 calories, this extraordinarily satisfying smoothie will keep you full all morning. It's a remarkable way to receive a boost of caffeine and more protein to keep you going till lunch.

Could you maybe arrive early at any point?

If you have any leftovers, you can store them in a covered bricklayer container and they will stay fresh for 24 hours in the refrigerator, but I advise drinking them right away. Simply recombine everything with a fork if the smoothie separates while being refrigerated in the unlikely event that it did.

What kind of coffee is best to use?

For this recipe, blended espresso works best; you can use your favorite brand. If you're sensitive, go ahead and use decaffeinated espresso, and if you like it, use a rich espresso.

CONCLUSION

The Glucose Goddess Cookbook is a comprehensive guide for making delicious, wholesome meals that support glucose control.

Along with practical advice on controlling glucose levels, it provides important information on understanding glucose and its impact on health.

The cookbook has a large number of dishes in a variety of categories, such as breakfast favorites, lunchtime favorites, evening indulgences, satisfying snacks, savory treats, and energizing beverages and refreshments.

The cookbook helps people make thoughtful selections to support stable glucose levels by emphasizing low-glycemic fixings, sound substitutes, and piece control.

It emphasizes the value of incorporating lean proteins, fiber-rich veggies, and healthy fats while reducing the use of added sweets and high-carbohydrate ingredients.

Additionally, the cookbook offers instructions on how to control blood sugar via steaming, grilling, baking, and sautéing. Additionally, it emphasizes the need for portion control and provides dinner preparation advice for creating balanced and satisfying feasts.

People who use the Glucose Goddess Cookbook's recipes and advice can enjoy delicious meals while improving their overall health and glucose control. This cookbook has something for everyone, whether you're looking for energizing breakfast options, satisfying lunch and dinner ideas, or indulgent yet glucose-accommodating pastries.

Make sure to speak with a registered dietician or medical services expert for personalized advice and direction based on your unique dietary needs and wellness goals. You can embark on a culinary adventure that sustains glucose management and improves your general prosperity with the help of the Glucose Goddess Cookbook.